THE LURE OF THE
JAPANESE GARDEN

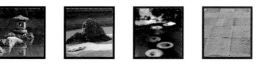

THE LURE OF THE
JAPANESE
GARDEN

ALISON MAIN &
NEWELL PLATTEN

Foreword by
Julie Moir Messervy

Wakefield
Press

Wakefield Press
17 Rundle Street
Kent Town
South Australia 5067

First published 2002

Designed by Dean Lahn, Lahn Stafford Design, Adelaide
Scanning by Hyde Park Press, Adelaide
Typeset by Clinton Ellicott, Wakefield Press, Adelaide
Printed and bound in Singapore by www.coloursymphony.com

National Library of Australia
Cataloguing-in-publication entry

Main, Alison.
The lure of the Japanese garden.

Includes index.
ISBN 1 86254 561 8.

1. Gardening, Japanese. 2. Gardening – Japan.
3. Japan – Description and travel.
I. Platten, Newell. II. Title.

712.0952

Government
of South Australia   A R T S A

Wakefield Press thanks Fox Creek Wines
and Arts South Australia for their support.

Title page: Kinkakuji, Kyoto.
Contents page 1: Isuien, Nara.
Contents page 2: Toji-in, Kyoto.

Contents

Foreword

Julie Moir Messervy

It was with a sense of trepidation that I first read *The Lure of the Japanese Garden*. I hoped it would not be yet another pretty picture book written by non-Japanese-speaking Westerners based on enthusiasm and secondary sources. What an agreeable surprise to find that it is the very book that I've always wanted to write for my travelling friends and colleagues: a guidebook, yes, but one that describes and delights in the contemporary Japanese context that surrounds each of these ancient works of landscape art. Alison Main and Newell Platten are insatiably curious travellers who collect garden experiences, just as I do. They note and comment upon the quirky, the silly, and the sublime, and explain all manner of details that matter to *gaijin* (foreigners) as they make their way through the bemusing twists and turns of Japanese society.

My own collecting expedition started in Japan some 25 years ago. I was there, thanks to a foundation grant, to study garden design under the tutelage of a then up-and-coming garden master named Kinsaku Nakane. My first assignment was to look at more than 60 gardens in and around Kyoto, most open to the public for a small fee – and all described in *The Lure of the Japanese Garden*. Every day for three months, another American student and I would meet at the Mister Donuts (pronounced 'Mista Donuts-sue') near the design studio and begin our day's journey across Kyoto on bikes, tram, or bus. We lugged along our cameras, sketch pads, and journals in order to document our findings, but Professor Nakane was specific about our task: Don't look at these gardens intellectually, but instead 'open your hearts to their beauty and meaning'. This was not easy to do for two Westerners. Inevitably, we would end up examining and evaluating what we saw – trying to understand how the designer would set a particular rock, teasing out the meaning behind its placement, analysing it as part of a compositional whole. We tried many ways to simply open our hearts: we'd sit Zazen (meditating in a lotus position) before visiting a garden or we would sketch what we saw; one day we even took a vow of silence for the day as we contemplated the dry landscapes before us. In the end, what taught us the most about the soul of a garden was to actually help build them ourselves. Hauling wheelbarrows of soil, pruning azaleas, watching Professor Nakane set stones, tamping down haircap moss – these activities allowed us to know the techniques employed over the centuries for building these three-dimensional masterpieces.

Other activities also added to my understanding of Japanese garden design. I lived in a traditional Zen Buddhist nunnery in the south-east part of Kyoto, with two nuns and several young male university students, where I had to speak Japanese. The temple had a small tea garden that Professor Nakane's garden crew maintained, connected to a rustic but elegant teahouse at the back of the property. There I learned the art of the tea ceremony. This ancient art taught me about spatial composition: how to place different objects – a ceramic tea bowl, a bamboo whisk, a metal tea kettle, a lacquerware tea caddy – next to each other in an aesthetic manner, invaluable concepts when I began to compose gardens myself, setting stones, trees, shrubs, and path elements in a harmonious way for my own clients.

On weekends and holidays, I enjoyed contemporary Kyoto life and culture, and, like Alison Main and Newell Platten, visited coffee houses, sake bars, public baths and noodle stalls. As they so well describe, the coffee houses offer a delightful interlude between garden viewing – each one designed as a special contemplative setting that takes you out of the hubbub of daily urban life for the time it takes to drink a cup of coffee. The inward-looking, finely detailed sensibility of these coffee houses, together with the accessible but private nature of the Japanese garden suggested the direction for my own work: to create contemplative places in cities, where people need them most.

Professor Nakane always told us that 'one art means all arts'. He meant that the art of tea ceremony, that of garden making, that of interior design all stem from the same basic ideas. This consistency of design principles can be found in the earliest Shinto shrine buildings through to the most over-the-top fashions or graphic design today. A fundamental design tenet resonates through Japan's thousand-year history: hold one attribute constant while another one changes. Thus we notice a long, rectangular paving stone path interrupted by a large, round stepping stone; a mud-and-wattle wall decorated with lines of horizontal roof tiles punctuated by curvy end caps of the same material; or a *tokonoma* in a Japanese house that inserts one rounded polished support post amidst the other hewn columns. This principle of continuity and change dovetails well with another design principle: refining nature to its most essential elements. Gardens are framed, ancient trees are bound with rice straw roping, a *sumie* painting's brushstrokes of ink suggest a moon rising over a mountain landscape. Surprisingly, in a country that is so densely populated, the beauty of nature can be found in the most unlikely of places: a restroom holds a vase with a tiny flower arrangement; a beautifully composed box lunch you buy on trains; the valuable tea bowls displayed by the local department store.

Always, paradox reigns. Is a tea-ceremony room bright or dark with its intimate scale and shadowy corners? Elegant or primitive with its rustic post alongside smooth *tatami* mats? Is the sandy 'sea' of a dry landscape garden moving or still? When you look at a miniature *bonsai* tree or a tray garden, are you tiny or huge in relationship to it? Such riddles delight and confound, engaging one's mind and senses in play. The ultimate principle of Japanese design is, of course, 'less is more'. Suggestion is always preferable to an outright statement. A single tree denotes a vast grove. One rock becomes a towering mountainscape. Things are not always what they seem.

These principles have inspired me throughout my life as teacher, lecturer, writer, and designer. Where specific Japanese garden conventions may not have been appropriate in a Western setting, the principles always remain inevitably right for every project. They are universals that bear translation from one culture to the next. Since those early days in Japan, I have continued to collect gardens; to discover what I can learn about design that can be turned into a new kind of garden through my own design efforts. I have come to love the symmetry of the French *parterre*, the axiality of the Mughal pleasure ground, the horticultural brilliance of the English landscape garden. I have delighted in discovering Tolstoy's musing places on his 3000-acre estate, Yasnaya Polyana, five hours south of Moscow.

My search has also taken me to Japanese-style gardens around the world. And they are everywhere! At Bellagio, on Lake Como in Italy, the Villa Melzi garden has a lake-and-islands stroll garden right beside its allee of pollarded plane trees. A fine Japanese garden in Wroclaw, Poland, possesses extensive streambeds, waterfalls and paved walkways among its azalea hillsides. Other gardens are more interpretive: in Paris, you can enjoy the Unesco Jardin Japonais, designed by Isamu Noguchi in 1958 (7, Place de Fontenoy, Paris 07 SP, France 75352, +33 (0) 1-45-68-10-00; www.unesco.org). A modernist Japanese garden, replete with Noguchi sculptures and pared-down plantings, the garden's features include a Peace Fountain and a meditation hall planned by Japanese architect Tadao Ando. Even Giverny's impressionist pond could be considered a Japanese garden as interpreted through the hazy eyes of Claude Monet (Claude Monet Foundation, rue Claude Monet 27620 Giverny; www.giverny.org). The grand willows weeping over a wisteria-clad bridge across a pond nearly overtaken by waterlilies could be seen as a romanticised version of some of the Imperial gardens in Kyoto.

My own garden *Sensei* (teacher) – Professor Nakane – created expansive Japanese gardens in many places including Singapore, Australia and China. Seiwa-en in Singapore is a huge Japanese garden built upon an island and linked by bridge to an equally huge Chinese garden on an adjacent island (1 Chinese Garden Road, Singapore 619795; www.singapore-ca.com). In the United States, Professor Nakane constructed a waterfall, rill and garden for former president Jimmy Carter's Library and Conference Center in Atlanta, Georgia (441 Freedom Parkway, Atlanta, GA 30307). Although this charming garden is only open to the public on certain days, visitors can view its pond and waterfall at all times. At the Museum of Fine Arts, Boston, Professor Nakane produced one of his last masterpieces: Tenshin-en, the Garden of the Heart of Heaven, which I was privileged to help design and manage as it was being built. Professor Nakane set the 283 stones of this half-acre dry landscape garden the day after he viewed New England from a small plane. I wanted to entice him to create a garden that reflected its regional setting, so we flew over Boston Harbor, Cape Cod, the Maine coast, the White Mountains and the Connecticut River valley so he could take in the beauty of these landscapes. The result is a garden that displays many of the traditional features of a Japanese garden: the Tortoise and Crane islands and the dry waterfall and pond, juxtaposed with edges that evoke islands off the Maine coast and the deep woods of New Hampshire. Professor Nakane created within the garden's confines, ' . . . the essence of mountains, the ocean and islands . . . as I have seen them in the beautiful landscape of New England'. (465 Huntington Avenue, Boston, MA 02115-5523, (617) 267-9300).

American readers who cannot travel to Japan can take a tour of some Japanese gardens in the United States. Some are traditional gardens that derive their ideas directly from Japanese garden conventions and methodologies. Others are more experimental in their approach. Following is a list, by no means exhaustive, of American gardens I have seen and enjoyed or have heard are worth exploring. Many more are to be found on the informative website www.jgarden.org.

I start in the Pacific North-west, whose climate most closely resembles that of Japan. This of course means that most of the same plants flourish here as do in Kyoto – an unfair advantage! My favourite Japanese garden in the United States is the Japanese Garden in Portland, Oregon. Founded as a nonprofit organisation in 1962 and maintained through admissions, memberships, special gifts and donations, the garden was designed in 1963 by Professor Takuma Tono and opened to the public in 1967. It offers five different garden styles set on five and one-half acres: you can enjoy the Strolling Pond Garden, the Natural Garden, the Dry Landscape Garden, the Flat Garden, and the Tea Garden. I love the *shakkei* or 'borrowed scenery' effect of a high vista from a viewing pavilion across the city of Portland towards the Cascade Mountains. This landscape is a must-see for all who love Japanese gardens. (Japanese Garden Society of Oregon, 611 S.W. Kingston Avenue, Portland, Oregon 97201; (503) 223-1321; www.japanesegarden.com).

The Japanese Garden of Seattle in the Washington Park Arboretum, sited on a pond, is described in their website as a 'compressed world of mountains, a forest, a lake, rivers, meadows, and a village'. Designed by Juki Iida in 1960, the garden has a tea house called the 'Arbor of the Murmuring Pines', a Moon-Viewing Stand and an Emperor's gate. (1502 Lake Washington Boulevard East, Seattle, WA 98112, (206) 684-4725; www.seattlejapanesegarden.org.)

Across the bay, on Bainbridge Island, lies the wonderful Bloedel Reserve (7571 NE Dolphin Drive, Bainbridge Island, WA 98110-1097; (206) 842-7631; www.bloedelreserve.org). Set in and among other gardens, including a woodland path, a bird sanctuary and a French country estate, the Japanese garden designed by Kawana Koichi is a *karesansui*, or dry landscape garden, that is built over a filled-in swimming pool fronting on a lovely viewing pavilion and backed up by billows of blooming azaleas. Nearby is the Moss Garden. A path follows a narrow rivulet through acres of moss, the closest experience to Kyoto's Saiho-ji that you can have outside of Japan. The path leads to a long rectangular pool surrounded by towering cedar trees. Here you can contemplate the sky, framed by the evergreens and reflected in the still waters of the clay-bottomed pool. Not so far away, in Vancouver, British Columbia, are the Momiji Gardens and the Nitobe Gardens at the University of British Columbia, both noted for their wonderful plantings so reminiscent of those in Kyoto. (Momiji Gardens, Hastings Park, Pacific National Exhibition, Renfrews Street and Hastings Street, Vancouver, BC; UBC Botanical Gardens, 6501 NW Marine Drive, Vancouver BC V6T 1Z4.)

Perhaps the most famous Japanese garden in America is the Japanese Tea Garden at Golden Gate Park in San Francisco. Initially built for the 1894 World Exhibition, it is the oldest public Japanese garden in California. No visitor will ever forget crossing the bright red Moon Bridge, climbing so high above the streambed below. (Tea Garden Drive and Martin Luther King Jr Drive, San Francisco, CA 94117, (415) 752-1171.)

Another important landscape is the Huntington Library Botanical Garden in San Marino (1151 Oxford Road, San Marino, CA 91108, (626) 405-2100; www.huntington.org). Sited in a small canyon, the Japanese garden sits isolated from the many other subgardens at Huntington. Built in 1911, it is one of the oldest and most mature Japanese gardens in America today. An older lake-and-islands garden joins together with a newer *karesansui* landscape; all surrounded by the other gardens of this old estate, among them Lily Ponds, a Desert Garden and Conservatory, a Palm Garden, Rose Garden, Camellia Garden and Shakespeare Garden.

In the south-west one finds a surprising number of Japanese-style gardens. The Denver Botanic Garden hosts a handsome Japanese garden, and Phoenix is building a Japanese Friendship Garden. Texas, San Antonio, Austin and Fort Worth all have Japanese gardens, and the Fort Worth Botanic Garden has a sizeable garden including a stroll garden, meditation garden, teahouse, *koi* pond, and moon-viewing deck.

The motto of the Missouri Botanical Garden's Seiwa-En is 'the garden of pure, clear harmony and peace'. As the largest traditional Japanese garden in North America, Seiwa-en covers fourteen acres, including a 4 1/2 acre lake surrounded by vast lawns and a meandering strolling path. Designed by Koichi Kawana, a distinguished professor of environmental design and landscape architecture at the University of California, Los Angeles, Professor Kawana supervised the construction and ongoing development of the garden until his death in 1990. Seiwa-en was dedicated in 1977. It is a *chisen kaiyu-shiki*, or 'wet strolling garden', a style developed by wealthy landowners of the late Edo period in nineteenth century Japan. (4344 Shaw Boulevard, St Louis, MO 63166-0299, (314) 577-5100; www.mobot.org).

Moving north, a wonderful Japanese garden may be found in Rockford, Illinois. The Anderson Gardens, built by John and Linda Anderson and designed by Hoichi Kurisu of Portland, Oregon, was created on the Anderson property around a natural spring-fed pond. Masahiro Hamada created the tea house and viewing house. The garden and the Anderson Center, where Japanese studies and horticulture are taught, are both open to the public. (318 Spring Creek Road, Rockford, Illinois 61107, (815) 229-9390; www.andersongardens.org.)

The gardens of David Slawson, author of *Secret Teachings in the Art of the Japanese Garden*, and fellow student of Professor Nakane, are also worthy of note. His small Japanese garden, *Jo Ryo En* – The Garden of Quiet Listening – is at Carleton College in Northfield, Minnesota (104 Maple Street, Northfield, MN 55057, (507) 646-4317). Highlighted for its 'grace, human scale, and contemplative atmosphere', the garden and small viewing pavilion offer a charming place for students and faculty to find solace and reflection. Other beautiful gardens by David Slawson are at the Cleveland Botanical Garden (11030 East Boulevard, Cleveland, OH 44106, (216) 721-1600) and the Garvan Woodland Gardens in Arkansas (540 Arkridge Road, Hot Springs National Park, AR 71903, (800) 366-4664;

www.garvangardens.org). This newly created Japanese-style garden, called 'Garden of the Pine Wind', features a majestic twelve-foot-high waterfall that cascades into a rock and stream garden, with a Japanese Maple Hill, a Full Moon Bridge and many other attractions.

A well-known garden in Delray Beach, Florida, is the Morikami Museum and Japanese Gardens, owned and operated by the Palm Beach County Department of Parks and Recreation (4000 Morikami Park Road, Delray Beach, Florida 33446, (561) 495-0233; www.morikami.org). Its website states that it is the only museum in the United States dedicated to the living culture of Japan. Its two hundred acres house gardens in two phases, with the first built around a seven-acre lake and waterfall and bonsai collection, and the second, newer gardens designed by Koichi Kawana to represent six periods of Japanese garden history.

In Washington, DC, the Hillwood Museum Gardens, the 25-acre former estate of Marjorie Merriweather Post, is being restored to its 1960s' condition by Zen Associates, a Boston-based Japanese garden design firm (4155 Linnean Avenue, NW, Washington DC 20008, (202) 686-5807; www.hillwoodmuseum.org). Other work by Zen Associates, run by Shinichiro Abe, another student of Professor Nakane, is in New York at the United Nations: The UN Peace Bell Garden (46th Street and 1st Avenue, New York 10017, (212) 963-8687) where members of the General Assembly gather on World Peace Day as the Secretary General rings the Peace Bell, cast from coins of sixty different countries. The garden is a beautifully wrought stone landscape that is worth visiting. Also in Manhattan, the Japan Society Gallery offers an elegant interior garden space as a respite from the workaday world (333 East 47th Street, New York, NY 10017, (212) 832-1155; www.jpnsoc.org).

Across the Brooklyn Bridge, visitors can delight in the renovations to the Brooklyn Botanic Gardens' Japanese Hill-and-Pond style garden (1000 Washington Avenue, Brooklyn, NY 11225-1099, (718) 622-4433; www.bbg.org). This garden, originally designed in 1914–15 by Takeo Shiota, is a masterpiece of cloud-pruning and quiet control. Its viewing pavilion and large vermilion *Torii* that rises out of the pond is simply and beautifully rendered. In Long Island City, in Queens, is the Isamu Noguchi Garden Museum (32–37 Vernon Boulevard. At 33rd Road, Long Island City, Queens, NY 11106-4926, (718) 721-1932; www.noguchi.org) – not so much a Japanese garden as a sculpture garden created by a Japanese sculptor. On exhibit in and around a converted factory building are more than 250 works by the sculptor, including a garden of granite and basalt sculptures. Outside New York City there are many Japanese-style gardens to enjoy. The John P. Humes Japanese Stroll Garden (Dogwood Lane, Mill Neck, NY 11765, (516) 676-4486) is a four-acre site in Mill Neck on Long Island. Designed by Stephen Morrell, the garden was acquired by the Garden Conservancy in 1993. At Innisfree (Tyrrel Road, Millbrook, NY 12545, (845)-677-8000; www.innisfreegarden.com) in Millbrook, the 180 acres designed by owner Walter Beck with landscape architect Lester Collins offer a marvellous mélange of Chinese, Japanese, Egyptian and Roman influences, with a distinctly North American flavour. The Hammond Museum's

Japanese Stroll Garden in North Salem is another charming mix of Japanese and American ideals (Deveau Road, North Salem, NY 10560, (914) 669-5033; www.hammondmuseum.org).

One of my very favourite Japanese-style gardens in this country is on Mount Desert Island in Maine. The Asticou Azalea Garden (Asticou Way, Seal Harbor and Peabody Drive, Northeast Harbor, ME 04662, (207) 276-3344; www.asticou@asticou.com). This charming landscape, owned and maintained by the Island Foundation, features more than twenty varieties of azaleas over 2.3 acres of strolling paths that lead the visitor past a stream, an iris pond and a meditation garden. The garden was created in part to preserve the plants from the Beatrix Farrand's shorefront estate called Reef Point. Designer Charles Savage bought Farrand's collection of plants after the Bar Harbor fire of 1947, and divided it between Asticou and Thuya Gardens, another must-see garden just up the road.

Every one of the settings I have visited has in turn influenced my own design thinking, as can be seen at the Toronto Music Garden that I designed with cellist Yo-Yo Ma (475 Queens Quay West, Toronto, (416) 338-0338; www.city.toronto.on.ca/parks/music_index.htm). In this three-acre park along the harborfront, we were inspired by the *First Suite for Unaccompanied Cello* by J.S. Bach, and used images, emotions and structure expressed in the music to create a garden of six 'movements' that are really different garden rooms that flow into one another. My use of Japanese principles of design – of continuity and change, paradox, abstraction of nature, and less is more – are evident throughout the twists and turns of the garden. Stones are placed in the Prelude section as a riverscape; in the Sarabande in the form of a snail shell; in the Gigue as a string of pearls. Plantings are exuberant but clear in their intent: the Allemande is host to a birch grove; the Courante to a wildflower meadow; the Minuet to a formal perennial border where performance happens on a circular stage.

To visit the gardens of Japan is to experience perhaps the most intense design experience found anywhere in the world, for each landscape offers the visitor a view of exquisite beauty combined with deep meaning. Once lured to visit Japanese gardens, you will never again see the world with the same eyes: you too will collect gardens wherever you go, in search of another landscape of richness, of perfection, of joy. *The Lure of the Japanese Garden* offers you a guide to just the right elements for your journey: a pathway of elegant prose, special events along the way – the 'intermissions' – that pique your interest and promote thought, and a point of view that is fresh, clear-seeing, and articulate.

Preface

Going to Japan at all was an accident. In 1985, our planned foray to India suddenly seemed fraught with too many surprise discomforts for a man with a back problem. Seduced by firm beds and sleekly efficient trains, we passed up the charm of Indian uncertainties for Japan's combination of practical ease and cultural fascination, and its contrast between the restraint of traditional culture and Tokyo-style glitz.

On that first trip together, we started looking at gardens almost by chance, just as pretty things to enjoy. Later we began to comprehend that whether beautiful, austere or eccentric, a Japanese garden always embodies meaning and significance beyond mere appearance – historic, symbolic, religious and meditative purpose, poetic and artistic allusion or a combination of meanings. The revelation of the gardens' beauty and conceptual dynamism has taken us back many times and led us into increasing research.

Setting out, we would have liked a guide to a garden's physical aspects and access that also introduced theoretical and aesthetic matters – a travel companion offering understanding of its main significance. Few books on Japanese gardens combined these topics with practical advice and portability, except for Treib and Herman's excellent *A Guide to the Gardens of Kyoto*, nor did they cover the country. As the heart of Japanese garden culture and site of the most magnificent examples, Kyoto is well documented, but for gardens further afield, we found ourselves collating information from many sources, following up small clues to new discoveries.

Eventually realising that our information covered a wide geographic area we decided to write the small garden guide that we would have welcomed in our early garden viewing, a book that might also act as a primitive introduction to Japanese culture. Wanting as well to share some of our odd pleasures in Japanese travel, we have included some more personal essays – 'intermissions' about our daily experiences. Our photographs of the gardens are totally 'as found' on ordinary visits without special arrangements. We wished to show the gardens as they are, without prior preparation and as anyone may photograph them. We have learnt a lot along the way, particularly that the best time to photograph gardens is in the rain, although holding an umbrella over the lens can pall. Knowing nothing about snow photography was expensive in terms of film. After the initial trips we graduated to Olympus 4ti cameras, valued for their spot metering.

Saihoji's moss garden, Kyoto.

Often we are asked if we have a Japanese garden, or people expect we might like to design one, but we feel that they are usually inappropriate to Australia's very different culture, climate and geography, except in association with projects of specific Japanese cultural interest. We wish to show the symbolic relationship of the Japanese garden to nature and philosophy so that the understanding of this framework may assist people elsewhere to develop new garden forms that express the cultural language and myths of their own country.

For us, Japan has become a place where we live, at least in our minds. We know enough about Japan to understand that our Japan is largely imaginary, never having lived there or progressed past being tourists, but its presence pervades our life in Adelaide and we are often homesick. A collection can be a question of personal ordering, of systematising a body of objects: ours is one of memories of gardens, one that we can only possess in the mind, but that we would like to share.

We would like to thank Professor Günter Nitschke for inspiration, advice and pleasant Kyoto interludes; he introduced us to many fascinating ideas. We are indebted to our friends at Wakefield Press for making it happen – for their initial belief, continuing help and assistance over seven years, and Lahn Stafford Design for their creative presentation. Albert Gillissen, Peter Ward, Tony Radford, Ann Newmarch and Ian North leapt to our help on request. Liz and Rob Read welcomed us in Odawara and share a certain state of mind. Midori Sakai is a great language teacher, but had the wrong pupil; the Contemporary Art Centre of South Australia gave support by publishing early versions of some essays in *Broadsheet*, and Adelaide's Japan Australia Friendship Association is a constant encouragement. We would like to thank our family and friends for patience.

Because our travels are intermittent and independent, we do not have friends in Japan to thank individually, but we want to thank the many Japanese people who have helped in every way imaginable, particularly those who open their beautiful gardens to visitors. So many brief acquaintances provided an extraordinary warmth of welcome.

Newell Platten and Alison Main, Adelaide 2002

Authors' Note

The gardens included are all open to the public daily from about 9 am to 5 pm, with the exceptions we indicate. Personal names are shown in the Japanese manner, with family name first, given names following. With compound words, we stay close to Japanese construction and map usage, only departing for needs of clarity or pronunciation. Thus the suffixes for temples '*ji*', '*dera*', are affixed (Tofukuji, Miidera) and the suffix for sub-temple '*in*' is hyphenated (Daisen-in, Konchi-in). Japanese words are explained in the text on first appearance and in the glossary. We do not repeat English equivalents for suffixes like '*ji*' (temple) as in Daitokuji temple. We do not distinguish between short/long o sounds with such conventions as *oo*, *ou*, or *oh* as they suggest inappropriate pronunciation in English. We apologise for any errors; they are entirely our own responsibility.

Gardens are located on maps in Chapter 9 by the garden number, showing the town on regional maps, and on the Kyoto map, garden positions. Excellent free maps are obtainable from Tourist Information Offices. Some maps are included for smaller cities, where information is not so readily available.

The poem on page 15 is reprinted from *A Waka Anthology, Volume One: The Gem-Glistening Cup*, translated with a Commentary and Notes by Edwin A. Cranston, published by Stanford University Press, 1993. The poem on page 23 is reprinted from *Chinese Poems*, Arthur Waley, George Allen and Unwin, London 1948, permission granted by Dover Publications. We thank Professor Günter Nitschke for permission to use quotes attributed to him. For other quotations we have made all efforts to obtain permission without response.

To Anna, Bronwyn and Tessa

. . . .

and in memory of
Marion and James Norman Main

GARDEN TRAVELS
A YEAR OF SEASONS

*E*very year or so we wander on and off trains, squeezing our bags into coin lockers and chatting about garden locations to serious girls in tourist information offices, hotel managers, the local police and a variety of people who leap out of the crowd to tell us about their holiday in Australia. Gardens and trains have defined our experience of Japan; the former a focus, the latter a quirky consequence. Fifteen years of garden collecting has led us a crab-wise dance, meandering off super-express *shinkansen* tracks into unexpected places. Many gardens barely mentioned in English guides have proved great local attractions, while choosing a town to stay in purely because of its central position has led to surprises like Kofu, the prosperous heart of the Japanese wine industry north of Mount Fuji. There, grapevines everywhere form a green tent at head height.

A multitude of well-signposted fast trains makes Japan one of the simplest countries for travel. English is usually found on main lines, but elsewhere most names appear in the phonetic syllabary *hiragana*. Just learning this is useful, even if you don't try *katakana*, the equivalent system for foreign words like *terebi* (television). On the station platform, if you can't check *kanji*, the Chinese characters, perfect timing ensures that if your ticket says 10 am, the train at ten is the one you want. The most enduring problem is finding the right car entry spot, essential for the ten-second stops. Car numbers dangle like washing along the platform awning.

Iwaki, Fukushima Prefecture: one-stop ride to find the peaceful retreat of Ganjoji. Grappling with luggage and undersized lockers among commuters' feet in a crowded little waiting room. Relaxing at last on the train's burgundy plush, we suddenly depart with a blast of Schubert's Trout, *abruptly truncated. Everyone immediately sleeps.*

We linger in Kyoto but speed from one regional garden to another. Only the JR railpass has enabled us to see so many gardens. Japan Railways, known as JR, is a linked system of companies that resulted from the 1987 privatisation of the previous loss-laden government organisation. Without a railpass to cover long distances our itineraries would be impossibly expensive and illogical. With normal fares our longest trip would have cost five times as much. Outside regular express routes, however, JR is not always the most useful way to go; more efficient routes are often non-JR lines, attracting a separate fare. Small trains often have great character and take eccentric routes through villages, even partly along town streets like the Enoden, a local line we took from Fujisawa to Kamakura.

In regional Japan our train rushes through a scenery of contrasts: urban fragments in a domestic mix with level plains of rice interspersed with abrupt hillsides clad with pines and bamboos. Orange groves, caterpillars of clipped tea bushes or a distant castle whizz past the window. Moving away from the vast Kanto/Kansai conurbations of central Honshu, the beauty of the country is still compelling. And yet, on the Japan Sea coast between the towns of Hagi and Matsue, the needle-bare limbs of the twisted pine trees on the coast suggest pollution. Many things are disturbing in this environment, but in places like Hikosan, in the mountains of Kyushu, distant valleys fall away towards the sea through clean air and birdsong, even if there is a regular bus every twenty minutes.

Winter, east of Lake Biwa: on a one-carriage local train from Kibugawa to Minakuchi through snow-blanketed rice fields, punctuated by hillsides of bamboos weighed down by leafy icicles. Here and there a red shrine in its small group of trees punctuates the flat white landscape. A crazy trip, but an early favourite – one of our first blind dashes into the countryside with only the name of town and temple, looking for Daichiji's great clipped hedge. The temple is closed because of 'an accident'. Probably snow damage to the hedge, we think, slushing back down a country lane between high icy banks.

The essence of winter is our long ride up the north sea coast. We walk in gusts of sleet among the ruins of Hagi castle, with its windswept stone ramparts and moats, while gale-scourged waves crash on the nearby beach. Outside the train window on a darkening afternoon, driving snowflakes veil white lumps of unknown machinery in railway yards. At Matsue castle, it's closing time; an old lady continues in a mild blizzard to sweep the weight of ice off surrounding hedges. Night falls. We walk in a mysterious toy town deserted in the snow. Next day we journey south to Takamatsu where, vanishing up into icy fog, Shiunsan looms over the great stroll garden of Ritsurin Park.

South of Matsue: in brilliant sunlight our train glides through snow-encrusted mountains, pine-tree boughs laden to the point of collapse with great icy loads. We are entranced, but the elderly couple next to us tenderly pull the blinds to shade their frill-bedecked sleeping grand-daughter from snow glare. Looking around, all blinds are down; the great nature love in Japanese hearts everywhere evinced on television is not in evidence. Further south we break our journey to see Raikyuji's great hedge. On the station platform at Bitchu-Takahashi, crocheted granny cushions warm the plastic shell seats.

Arriving for our first spring visit, we already know that catching a seasonal moment in Japan is uncertain. Blossom travels in a wave up the country, with television updates on its location. The ephemeral existence of cherry blossom being the ultimate metaphor for the transience of life, we think we may miss full bloom. Emerging from our hotel after a late Tokyo arrival we step out to the morning sight of a splendid sweep of blossom draped over a city wall. Ueno Park's avenue of trees is so thick with clouds of icy pink cherry blossom that the sky above is lost. Crowds stroll in a chattering dream; picnickers on a patchwork of blue plastic groundsheets await the night's carousal. On our later travels through a countryside of misty rain, an extravagance of blossom drifts over rows of trees along roads and river banks. Spring in Japan is white skies, moody greys and sharpest pale pink. *Sakura* bring light to drab spring days.

The ancient branches of huge trees form flowering canopies over elaborate bamboo trellises, gracing formidable temples like Miidera above Lake Biwa or Horyuji at Nara. The blooming of the great tree just beyond the aged wall of Ryoanji transforms the severity of the enigmatic stone garden, while on a magical morning at Arashiyama, in the west of Kyoto, trees along the river are clouds of brilliance in clear cold sun.

Kenrokuen, Kanazawa: cherries arch over a stream flowing with tender green spikes of young iris. Outside on the entry road between castle and garden, the admiring throng is constantly joined by grander arrivals emerging from white-laundered cab interiors. We gaze down at settings prepared for evening parties in the former castle moat, overhung by a flush of blossom. Ahead the vast remaining gate twists up into the university, an anticlimax.

In summer we speed cross-country through northern forests and the fresh green of young rice, in a countryside dotted with strings of paper carp frolicking over the fields. Rural Japan has solitude: a solitary fisherman standing on the edge of a rock strewn stream, a bicycle meandering along the narrow verge of a rice paddy. Valleys open out into patches of tilled land; rice fields everywhere emphasise the importance of rice cultivation to the country's spiritual ethos aside from economics. Over-production is creating problems for tiny village communities. As the quotas decline so do the ageing populations of isolated hamlets and their reasons for existence.

Moving west from Furukawa in northern Honshu: on a gloriously sunny morning we set off on the Rikuu Tosen Line towards Sakata. Small family vans on Sunday outings progress decorously alongside on the highway. Hikers on the slowly climbing train get out as the mountains start. Long tunnels, brief glimpses of steep gorges, sudden bridges and twists of river. Beside a station, wild azalea, fruit trees and wisteria tumble down an embankment. Later we descend gradually to the coast through rolling hills with tall pines. From Obori we see snowy peaks; in Sakata our hotel view over the train tracks is a great snow-crested mountain. Hidden thereafter in cloud.

In fiction, Tohoku, in the north of Honshu, has a rugged reputation for remote mystery and country ways, long winter hardship and ascetic mountain priests known as *yamabushi*, but for us it is the place to see May and summer flowers.

In the Dewa Sanzan area near Tsuruoka, we stroll from the Mt Haguro bus to Gyokusenji along a straight road between sky-filled rice fields, gleaming pale-blue between yellow flowers. Cloud reflections ripple in a cold breeze as we approach the pine trees screening a few modern village houses. Here lies the temple garden, all in flower. The priest's pretty young wife makes us tea, teaching us the word for primula – *kurinso*, the temple's emblem. South of the plain near Tsuruoka, mountain ranges run fingers right down to the sea's edge and narrow huddles of houses and fields squash into slits of valleys. Glimpses of the coast flash between tunnels until the land opens out towards Niigata where, five minutes after arrival, we leave our bags at a business hotel and find ourselves upstairs next-door in a bright coffee shop.

In June's wet season, summer shows Matsue's warmer face and we return mainly to see the Adachi Museum in the countryside not far away, with its expansive and wonderfully kept gardens viewed only from the orchestrated sequence of museum windows. Next day we set off in a one-carriage train to circle coastal Lake Shinji, leaving from Matsue Onsen station, a wooden relic from the twenties. Chatting to two women holidaying from the north, we curve along the northern lake edge, in and out of villages, along reedy shores, through damp misty fields to Hirata. The station is devoid of information, but outside we find a classic nine-seater coffee shop, whose ancient owner, communing with a friend over morning television, appoints himself as Hirata's tourist officer. After visiting Kokokuji we continue west through fields with pines planted as giant windbreaks; on the way changing on to an ancient train with a wooden floor and wire luggage racks that seem definitely pre-war. On arrival so does the eccentric station of Izumo-taisha-mae with its shiny tiled dome, coloured glass and timber trussed platform roof, sufficiently decrepit to attract a photographer. (So do we, odd-looking *gaijin* – 'outside people', foreigners.) We climb the hill to Izumo Taisha, the country's oldest Shinto shrine, a place of misty grandeur where mossy roofs loom against clouds and shifting drizzle while a sonorous bell booms.

Toyohashi, south-east of Nagoya: through narrow bamboo-lined cuttings, a single-carriage train (number 26 this trip) takes us to Makayaji in Mikkabi, a clean-cut temple garden with rocks set among smooth green grass. Moving on to find Ryotanji with its sweeps of azalea bushes, we relax on the next train, constantly glimpsing the waters of coastal Lake Hamana. The stop we request doesn't exist. (Try looking for a village called Inasa in a larger area called Inasa. Hard to explain. Or another time – Tokoji, in the Kofu suburb named after the temple. 'Yes! Here is Tokoji . . .') Friendly passengers help us buy the right ticket and put us on the bus. We spend a tranquil day of summer roaming.

Of all the Japanese seasons the most spectacularly beautiful is autumn, but it is almost harder to catch at its peak than spring. Throughout October a changing tapestry of colour begins to warm the hills; about 10 November the crowds declare autumn even if it hasn't arrived yet, and jaunt off to spots where it may be early.

By 30 November, it is officially over. One year, delayed till then, we speed to Kyoto hoping for autumn colour but resigned to our lateness. Autumn arrives three weeks late . . . the luckless people who were on time have gone home.

Red rivers of maple cascade down to the pond at Chishaku-in. Gingkoes thrust their shocking yellow against blue skies. Neat drifts of red leaves carpet ochre-dry grass at Sento Gosho, the old palace, while the quiet hermitage of Shisendo blazes with afternoon light and maple glow. Patches of scarlet and orange splash across mountainsides above our *shinkansen* as it hurtles to Hiroshima. We cross in a ferry to Miyajima to see the shrine of Itsukushima where wafts of foliage match its watery vermilion reflections and further out in the bay, the poster-famous giant red *torii*.

Miyajima 6 am: freezing at dawn's low tide, we walk out over mud to the great red torii. *Coins stud its barnacled grain, orange paint encrusted. Sounds of trickling water in the half-dark, the tide still ebbing. A heron beyond the breakwater. Houses still grey and sleepy. A villager slips across the draining bay in a short cut to work. Lanterns glow in the shrine, someone stirring within. On the bank hands clap, a man at prayer. Slowly light grows behind the mountain. An early business tour runs out to the* torii, *icy feet stamp for a moment or two, then leave. Mainland murmurs gently intensify. Just after eight the sun slants down the misty hillside to fire the gate in crimson incandescence. After breakfast, as we sail away, it fades into sun-filled mist, a dream before disappearance.*

The stroll garden is a perfect analogy for travel because not only is it often constructed as a series of references to famous views reminiscent of Hiroshige and other masters of the Japanese print, but it also acts as a journey whose engaging snares lure you along a mysterious path that twists and turns to place you before the next unexpected but carefully planned delight. A swoop of rising path lifts your eyes to a distant pagoda lantern framed by a pendant wisp of maple, but turns you back among banks of azaleas and high camellias to emerge on top of a small hill above a tranquil lake that narrows back to a canopied bridge. All this happens in a relatively small space, an appropriate metaphor for travel in Japan, where you can pass rapidly from verdant country fields and forest-covered mountains to the pinball gambling of *pachinko*, concrete castle reconstructions and the Moorish love-hotel fantasies of soapland.

At Kyoto, the Haruka express to Kansai airport is being cleaned by nattily uniformed girls. Like synchronised swimmers they move through in pairs rubbing armrests and window sills. Finally they waltz the seats round in duos to face the new direction and let us in. 1998 train number 52.

THE LANGUAGE OF GARDENS

Autumn at Nanzenji Hojo.

A limitless realm of imagination exists within the microcosm of the Japanese garden. Many gardens symbolically express ideas and places that have inspired or moved Japanese people over centuries, and very often the Chinese before them. Garden concepts may be based on myths or religious beliefs, the human desire for immortality, or notions of the structure of the universe and its relationship to human beings. Gardens may portray the grandeur of nature in miniaturised interpretations of vast oceans and landscapes, at times quite literally as in the large seventeenth-century Suizenji Park where a series of undulating mounds climax in a scaled-down Mt Fuji. More often they take on the idealised forms found in many Zen gardens. An occasional design may be abstracted to the point of enigma, as in the stone garden at Ryoanji, where an arrangement of fifteen rocks in a bed of gravel defies every interpretation it encourages.

Rocks play one of the most important roles in conveying meaning in Japanese gardens. They act as metaphors for the supernatural in spirits and deities, the natural in creatures, mountains, islands and waterfalls, and the man-made in boats and bridges. This widespread use may have originated in ancient mysticism, wherein ancestors and exceptional natural phenomena were revered for being invested with *kami*, or supernatural spiritual powers.

Natural phenomena included living beings and awe-inspiring objects such as the sun, mountains, rivers, caves, great trees and particular rocks whose significance might be identified by isolation within cleared spaces and binding with knotted ropes. When the first garden builders came to represent venerated objects such as mountains, they might naturally have sought out expressive rocks for the purpose. Again, the earliest gardens in Japan were inspired by those of China, with its older history of symbolic and sculptural use of rocks. In whatever way these origins may have conferred archetypal status, the longevity of rock formations has enabled preservation and reconstruction, so that a garden may have a longer life than its fragile associated buildings.

Underlying the pictorial qualities of Japanese gardens are thematic structures whose meanings have been made more accessible to westerners in recent years through the research and writings of scholars like Itoh Teiji, Loraine Kuck, Günter Nitschke and others. Meanings are revealed in what might be called a sign language, and here we outline cultural influences and symbols pertaining to gardens, seeking to establish an elementary vocabulary for 'reading' the gardens illustrated in this guide. The material has a chronological structure but themes, having been introduced, are followed for the course of their development which might take place over several historical periods. This involves some chronological leap-frogging; for a straightforward guide to historical and garden developments, see chapter 9.

The Plane and the Picturesque

In 607 AD, several years before construction began on the first garden in Japan actually recorded, a group of Japanese envoys arrived at Luoyang, the Chinese eastern capital during the reign of Emperor Sui Yang-ti. At the time the emperor's pleasure park, known as Western Park, was being built. Even by the standards for imperial excess set by previous rulers the construction of this park was an extraordinary endeavour.

At the Kazenomiya auxiliary sanctuary, dedicated to the *kami* of winds and part of the Outer Shrine complex, a small shelter covers the 'heart pillar' in an expanse of pebbles. Unlike Ise's main shrines, auxilliary shrines can be photographed.

Western Park, with a perimeter measuring 120 kilometres (75 miles), consumed the labour of a million labourers. Half of them died as they toiled digging a great system of lakes (the largest about 21 kilometres (13 miles) around) and waterways, and building mountains, islands, pavilions, colonnades, towers, terraces and sixteen luxurious palaces dispersed along shorelines. Plants, trees, birds and beasts were commandeered from nearby estates to stock the vast domain. Fully grown forest trees were uprooted and transplanted. Each palace had its own elaborate private garden to amuse the twenty resident imperial concubines, and each could only be approached over water by an imperial barge, its prow curled up in the head of a dragon or a mythical phoenix, its occupants enjoying the beauty and invention of each passing scene.

Western Park represented a tradition in the creation of imperial hunting parks and private pleasure gardens over one thousand years old. The visitors from the still-primitive Japan must have been astounded even by the unfinished work. In accordance with other contemporary cultural developments, it followed naturally that early ornamental gardens in Japan adopted Chinese precedents, incorporating artificial mountains, ponds and islands.

As an indigenous tradition took root and strengthened, gardens assumed a distinctive Japanese character while still containing those basic elements. Gardens began to include allusions to scenes that nobles and priests encountered as they travelled around the country or overseas. So deeply impressive were sea voyages that the ponds in most early gardens included pebbled, rock-strewn shorelines simulating coastal scenery, while trees are still manipulated to resemble the gnarled, windswept pines that so dramatically cling to headlands and islets. Some writers connect the pebble areas found in Japanese gardens throughout all subsequent historical periods to these early coastal scenes.

Another line of reasoning links these gravel spaces with indigenous spiritual beliefs and practices most profoundly expressed in the imperial shrines at Ise in Mie prefecture. The imperial line was believed by mythological account to have descended from the sun deity, Amaterasu Omikami. The deity's spirit, represented by a mirror, is enshrined in the Naiku (Inner Shrine) at Ise. Since the reign of Emperor Temmu (reigned 673–686 AD), both inner and outer shrines at Ise have been rebuilt every twenty years (a few lapses apart) on one of two adjoining sites. Glimpsed by ordinary

Snow lies on grooves of raked sand
at Daisen-in.

people over four layers of protective fencing, the current shrine buildings are arranged in a hierarchical and geometric order, reflecting Chinese planning principles while taking their architectural forms from indigenous elevated rice granaries constructed in the Yayoi period (200 BC–250 AD). Each unused site remains a plane of white pebbles, empty apart from a small shelter covering a sacred pillar whose replacement marks the culmination of the next rebuilding cycle. These silent, open spaces within dense, enclosing cryptomeria forests are climactic manifestations of a theme repeated time and again over the course of Japan's cultural development, with particular relevance to gardens.

The precursors of Ise's pebble-strewn spaces are thought to have been settings for devotional rituals practised in times before permanent shrines were built, places where people made supplication to spirits that could affect their lives for good or ill. The earliest may have been sanctified forest clearings around trees thought to be the abode of *kami*. Günter Nitschke, in his book *Japanese Gardens*, speculates that pebble-strewn precincts found at most Shinto shrines have evolved from temporary sacred enclosures set up on riverbanks to worship the sun deity at the beginning of each rice season. Rice granaries might themselves have been the nuclei of purified zones set within gravel spreads and the settings for religious rites conducted by chieftains. As Nishi Kazuo and Hozumi Kazuo note in *What is Japanese Architecture?* there were 'close connections between custodianship of food, divine sanction and temporal power'.

After the country became unified under the dominance of the Yamato kingdom from the fourth century AD, ultimate spiritual authority was assumed by emperors who presided over both religious and civic ceremonies. Spreads of gravel before palaces accommodated assemblies of ministers, aristocrats and officials, while at other times serving as settings for sacred rituals. Such spaces can be seen today at the Imperial Palace in Kyoto. There, a vast plane of white gravel forms the forecourt to the Shishinden, the great hall of state where coronations were conducted. A smaller courtyard before the Seiryoden, the ceremonial banquet hall since the mid-Heian period, at times acted as a purified zone for the ritualised descent of gods.

Illustrations of mansions built by Heian-period (794–1185) noblemen show how the Chinese style of garden and the indigenous tradition became integrated. In a typical example the courtyard south of the *shinden* or 'hall for sleeping' was, like the palace courtyard, spread with gravel for ceremonies and entertainments. Beyond lay a pond with one or more islands connected by bridges, and a hill made from excavated earth planted with trees. As Itoh Teiji points out in his book *The Gardens of Japan*, the Japanese word for the prototypal garden, *teien*, expresses this dual nature. *Tei*, being the courtyard space before a palace, refers to the gravel plane and *en* refers to the planted area.

Many Zen gardens, where the gravel planes no longer have any practical purpose but exist for aesthetic and intellectual reasons, show further stages of this evolutionary pattern. Gardens on the south side of *hojo*, or chief priest's quarters, were formerly entrance courts until the Muromachi period (1392–1568) when porches were added. While freed entirely for garden-making, some retain the previously essential gravel plane with little more than decorative patterns added; others are embellished with rocks and/or plants. Over time, and with original functions buried deep in history, the gravel plane has persisted as a design element, part of a garden-maker's vocabulary.

The wave-patterned gravel plane at Konchi-in, built in 1632, may symbolise water but its main role seems spatial. The plane holds a composition of islands and clipped bushes a comfortable viewing distance from the temple's verandah, in the way viewing a painting in a gallery requires a particular distance. This establishes a two-dimensional pictorial effect that is reinforced from inside the temple when the viewer sees the garden's three main focal points: the *kamejima* (turtle island), the *tsurujima* (crane island) and a central lantern/prayer stone composition separately framed by axially related openings in the external shoji (sliding paper screens).

Mystic Isles where Immortals Dwell

According to ancient Chinese mythology, somewhere east of the Chinese coast there were once five verdant and mountainous islands, each borne on the backs of three giant sea turtles. At some time a monster had devoured six turtles, leaving three islands known as P'eng-lai, Ying-chou and Fang-chang, and on these islands men and women who had gained immortality lived together in harmony. They dwelt in halls of gold, silver and jade amid trees dripping with pearls and other gems, dined on magic fruits and could take to the air on the backs of cranes. The three islands became the goals of voyages of discovery as Chinese emperors launched unsuccessful expeditions to obtain for themselves the elixir of eternal youth.

The failures of his predecessors persuaded Emperor Han Wu-ti (reigned 140–87 BC) to build a garden simulating the mythical islands in the hope that the immortals would be lured there and reveal to him the secrets of immortality.

Konchi-in's turtle island with its ancient withered cypress.

Horai composition at Ryogen-in.

Tsurujima at Makayaji, Mikkabi.

Near the Ch'ien Chang palace he created two large lakes containing islands shaped with the aid of rugged rocks into peaks and crags. On the islands he planted trees in spirit groves, herbs and flowers to bloom throughout the year. He built palaces so sumptuous that the immortals would mistake them for their own.

While Emperor Wu probably died disappointed, he achieved immortality of a kind. The ancient myth and the story of his garden were absorbed into the iconography of eastern gardens, to be recreated again and again over the centuries. In Japan the original three islands were condensed into one, known as Horai or Horaisan (Mt Horai), symbolised as *horai* mountain, *horai* island or *horai* rock, and often referred to as 'isle of the immortals'.

Turtles and cranes themselves came to symbolise immortality and feature in many gardens as turtle or crane islands. *Kamejima*, turtle islands, are the more easily distinguished; their mounded forms, raised heads, flippers and tails are often quite graphically depicted by the selection and placement of appropriately allusive rocks. *Tsurujima*, crane islands, may have extended necks, as in the garden of Makayaji, or tall rocks or plants suggesting wings. Turtle and crane peninsulas, *kamedejima* and *tsurudejima*, are frequently attached to pond edges.

The Mountain at the Centre of the Universe

The introduction of Buddhism to Japan, officially in the sixth century AD but earlier through natural cultural interchange with the mainland, led to knowledge of a cosmology found in Indian Buddhist teachings. According to this cosmology, a vast mountain known as Mt Meru and inhabited by supernatual beings lay at the centre of the world. Seven mountain ranges lay around Mt Meru in concentric circles, separated by seas or oceans with magical properties. Beyond the seventh circular range lay a great salt ocean containing four continents and eight islands, all inhabited by humans. An eighth mountain range made of iron, known as the Cakravada, encircled the salt ocean. All these mountains and oceans rested on a cylindrical

Shumisen at Mampukuji, Masuda.

foundation made up of layers of earth, gold, water and wind descending to a base of ether, or space, that stretched away indefinitely in all directions and contained an infinite number of similar worlds.

In 612 AD a Korean immigrant craftsman was engaged by Empress Suiko of the Yamato Court to build a 'Bridge of Wu' – a Chinese-style high-arched, red-lacquered bridge – and a miniature Mt Meru in the southern garden of the Imperial Palace. This is both the first record of a garden in Japan and the introduction of a symbol found in many subsequent gardens. Mt Meru, known as Shumisen in Japanese, is often prominent as a tall single rock, but is more recognisable when seen surrounded by subsidiary rocks in a concentric arrangement, as at Mampukuji in Masuda.

Cosmological Ordinances

When the Japanese of the seventh century adopted the institutions and systems of government pertaining to the T'ang dynasty they gained access to a rationale long established in China for the behaviour and organisation of the universe, and rapidly assimilated its tenets. A central belief in a dynamic interrelationship between man and nature caused the universe to be seen as a harmonious whole wherein man, heaven and earth constantly interacted in all aspects of existence.

From perhaps as early as 1000–500 BC, Chinese cosmologists had believed that events were produced and controlled by the interaction of two complementary principles: *yin*, female, passive, dark, and *yang*, male, active, bright. *Yin* and *yang* were not seen as intractable opposites but, like two sides of a spinning coin, mutually dependent and reciprocating in endless cycles of change.

Phenomena were understood in terms of *yin/yang* and a system of correlations based on 'Five Elements', namely wood, fire, earth, metal and water. The five elements are often referred to as 'Five Phases' or 'Five Operational Qualities', names thought better to describe their dynamic and interactive qualities through their cycles of 'Mutual Creation', as in wood producing fire, and 'Mutual Destruction', as in water overcoming fire. The theory of Five Elements correlates each element extensively with known events, objects and sensations, such as seasons, directions, human organs, tastes, emotions, colours and creatures. Fire, for example, correlates with summer, south, heart, bitter, joy, red, and hairy creatures. By such correlations, correspondences between natural events and human affairs could be inferred.

Literally translated as 'wind and water' and known as Chinese geomancy in western writings, *feng-shui* constitutes a system of divination whereby dwellings for both the living and the dead are sited to accord with natural powers and so most auspiciously serve the well-being of their occupants. The fundamental aim is to locate a dwelling with proper regard for the functioning of *yin* and *yang*; each primal force said to be manifest in the earth's topography and present in 'breaths' (*ch'i*), or streams or currents in the earth's crust and atmosphere. The *feng-shui* practitioner's compass is an elaborate tool that correlates all the factors that must be considered if there is to be, as Laurence Thompson notes in *Chinese Religion: An Introduction*, a 'tranquil harmony of all the heavenly and terrestrial elements which influence that particular spot'. It arranges, in up to twenty-four concentric rings around a central 'heaven pool', a bewildering array of information, such as the eight trigrams and the sixty-four hexagrams of the *I-Ching*, the five elements, configurations of the lunar and solar systems, stars, planets, seasons and so on. Thompson argues that the very complexity of *feng-shui* sustained its credibility: a family's bad luck following site selection could be attributed to faulty interpretation rather than the 'pseudo-science' itself.

For all its apparent mysticism, *feng-shui* has been tied to sensible environmental practices. For example, supernatural creatures were believed to inhabit compass cardinal points: 'black turtle' north, 'azure dragon' east, 'red phoenix' south and 'white tiger' west. Propitious siting of a dwelling would require the tiger right and the dragon left, so that it faces south towards winter sunlight. The tiger and the dragon could be traced in the outlines of hills and mountains, with the dragon's limbs and arteries discernible in chains of hills and winding rivers. To ensure prosperity and honour, a dwelling or tomb should be sited so that vital breath accumulating near the dragon's waist should not be allowed to dissipate fruitlessly east or west, and water should drain off in a tortuous winding course. In practice this meant protecting the back and sides of a dwelling, a tomb or a city with mountains or hills on the north, east and west sides, the directions in China of winter winds and invaders. Walls, hedges or buildings could substitute for mountains when appropriate. Land, or structures, with these auspicious *feng-shui* attributes might be likened to a prospective embrace – a body with arms outstretched to shelter or protect a child.

Historians observe that the Japanese people either never fully understood or deliberately misinterpreted many facets of philosophies imported from China, enabling them to graft an alien culture on to indigenous systems of belief and behaviour without destabilisation. Itoh Teiji, for example, relates a passage from the eleventh-century garden-making treatise known as the *Sakuteiki* where the writer, Tachibana no Toshitsuna, in proposing a suitable site for a dwelling in accordance with *feng-shui* principles, arbitrarily substitutes various tree groups for topographical features. Nevertheless, these ancient principles have endured, just as the polarities of *yin* and *yang* still seem deeply embedded in codes and aesthetic perceptions where opposing values may be freely and fully realised in harmonious conjunction.

Clipped bushes and angular building profiles contrast with soft background foliage at Shisendo.

Yin and *yang*, interpreted as the interdependence of opposites, finds expression in nearly all Japanese gardens, and indeed may be seen as the rationale underlying all design. It appears most pervasively as a contrast between the right-angled geometries of architecture and the free forms of gardens, as well as often between garden elements themselves. The composition of the garden at Makayaji presents rugged, hard, almost phallic, rocks dramatically imposed on sensuously curved, smooth, feminine grassy mounds. At Shisendo, clipped, rounded and tightly controlled azalea bushes stand out against a luxuriantly undisciplined mass of maple foliage; both elements are separated from the building by a plane of white sand and viewed within rectangular frames formed by roofs, floors and posts. The juxtaposition of these several contrasting layers, independently unremarkable, produces one of the most beautiful small gardens in Japan.

Gardens in Classical Japan

Before the creation of Nara as capital of ancient Japan in 710 AD, the palace had been moved after each emperor died in accordance with the belief that death pollutes a dwelling. In a site favoured geomantically, and near the important

Buddhist temples of Horyuji (founded 607) and Yakushiji (founded 680), the first permanent capital was laid out in the manner of the great Chinese city of Ch'ang-an (now Xi'an). A grid of streets ran in north–south and east–west directions, and the imperial palace compound lay at the north. In this new city, under the inspiring influence of a rich foreign culture, religion, scholarship and the arts flourished in what historian George Sansom describes as an 'almost magical growth of taste and skill' that has been 'rarely excelled or even equalled in any other country'.

Korean and Chinese craftsmen constructed gardens featuring ponds with islands, rock groupings, trees and flowering shrubs. Little remains of Nara gardens and, some recent reconstructions aside, most impressions are gained from a collection of over four thousand poems known as the *Man'yoshu* (Collection of Myriad Leaves). Although poems in the *Man'yoshu* predominantly dwell on human relationships, emotions and the beauties of landscapes, occasional fragments touchingly illuminate garden scenes across the seasons, as in this verse composed by high-ranking court official Otomo no Sukune Yakamochi (c 718–785) in 758:

> *Here along the pond*
> *Its reflection blooms again*
> *Down in the water –*
> *Come, pluck the shining ashibi*,*
> *Strip its flowers into your sleeves!*

*Ashibi is andromeda, a flowering plant with pendulous white blossoms.

In 794 the capital was relocated to a new site where the present city of Kyoto stands. Heiankyo, as the city was then named, was built in a broad valley enclosed by mountains on east, north and west sides, opening out and sloping gently to the south. Mt Hiei, lying in the north-east quarter, guarded the city from evil spirits thought to come from that direction. The original city plan was, like Nara, modelled on Ch'ang-an with a street grid oriented to the cardinal points and the imperial palace located at the northern end of its central north–south axis.

The architectural style of the Heian period (794–1185) ruling-class residence restated the embracing form, noted earlier, at an architectural scale. The style is known as *shinden* after the name given to the main central room at the base of the U. Open east–west corridors connected the *shinden* to flanking halls, completing the base, and from these halls covered walkways extended southwards to complete the U-shape and terminate in small pavilions, one known as the spring pavilion, the other as the fishing pavilion. Both these pavilions stood at the edge of a garden pond. Between the pond and the *shinden* lay the sparsely planted, gravel-spread inner courtyard. A stream should enter the site from the north or east, flow along the eastern side of the inner courtyard, enter the pond from the east and leave flowing westwards to wash away any evil spirits that had found their way into the house or garden.

For a delightful sense of the mood and substance of a Heiankyo garden we turn to *The Tale of Genji*, the classic novel of courtly life written by Murasaki Shikibu (c 975–c 1025). In connection with a boating party in the spring garden of another Murasaki, granddaughter of a former emperor, she writes:

> *The dragon and phoenix boats were brilliantly decorated in the Chinese fashion. The little pages and helmsmen, their hair still bound up in the page-boy manner, wore lively Chinese dress and everything about the arrangements was deliciously exotic, to add to the novelty, for the empress's women, of this south-east quarter. The boats pulled up below a cliff at an island cove, where the smallest of the hanging rocks was like a detail in a painting. The branches caught in mists from either side were like a tapestry, and far away in Murasaki's private gardens a willow trailed its branches in a deepening green and the cherry blossoms were rich and sensuous. In other places they had fallen, but here they were still at their smiling best, and along the galleries wisteria was beginning to send forth its lavender. Yellow yamabuki reflected on the lake as if about to join its own image. Waterfowl swam past in amiable pairs, and flew in and out with twigs in their bills, and one longed to paint the mandarin ducks as they coursed about in the water. Had that Chinese woodcutter been present, he might well have gazed on until his ax handle rotted away. Presently it was evening.*

All that now remains of the original imperial palace garden, once the finest and largest in the ancient capital, is Shinsenen (Divine Spring Garden), a small pond garden in central Kyoto. Only this quiet fragment recalls the hills, lakes and islands dotted with red-lacquered pavilions – a 13-hectare (33-acre) setting for boating excursions, banquets, dancing exhibitions, wrestling matches and other aristocratic amusements.

The Osawa Pond, now attached to Daikakuji, a temple in Kyoto's western foothills, was originally part of the country estate of retired Emperor Saga, built about 823. Between two islands, still visible and above water levels now

Shoseien's pond reflects a modern symbol – the Kyoto Tower.

higher, is one of a chain of five 'night mooring stones', a linear arrangement of rocky islets characteristic of the Heian period but of unclear origins and meaning. Meanwhile, just north of the Kyoto railway station on a site which fits descriptions of the Riverbank Villa built by Minamato no Toru, Minister of the Left, about 872, Shoseien nestles among anonymous apartments and office buildings. Rambling, relaxed and cheerfully unpristine, Shoseien still contains islands in its lake that include rock groupings said by scholar Loraine Kuck to be in 'typical Heian style'. These are faint traces of the first flowering of Japanese architectural and garden splendour, a time still seen as a golden age and prime cultural source.

Amida's Western Paradise

The graceful pond-mirrored pavilions of Byodo-in's Phoenix Hall, at Uji near Kyoto, present one of the loveliest sights in Japan today. For Fujiwara Yorimichi, who was *kampaku* (chief adviser to the emperor) and its creator in 1053, the hall housing the gilded image of Amida Buddha was the focal point of an earthly recreation of Amida's Western Paradise, or Pure Land (Jodo).

Serene reflections on an autumn day at Byodo-in, Uji.

Throughout the preceding classical era Buddhist teachings had been esoteric in form, accessible to the literate and the leisured, the priests and the nobility. Indeed, the Shingon Sect of Buddhism, with its emphasis on the emotional appeal of colours, patterns and ritual, had been popular in the aesthetically preoccupied court and a potent force behind the great classical flowering of the arts. The latter part of the tenth century and beyond was, however, a time of political uncertainty and disenchantment with established sects, which were too often sources of disorder, bloodshed and corruption. Also there was widespread belief that the world would soon be entering the time of Mappo (Latter Day of the Holy Law), when Buddha's authority would no longer prevail and a degenerate epoch would follow.

The times were ready for a simple comforting faith. This was supplied by the monk Genshin (942–1017), later called Eshin, who through his work *Essentials of Salvation* drew attention to a form of worship with a long history in Japan and China known as Nembutsu (Buddha Calling). Genshin taught that the recitation of the simple prayer 'Namu Amida Butsu' ('Homage to Amida Buddha') would invoke the compassion of Amida (Buddha Amitabha), and ensure the transport of believers' souls to an afterlife of everlasting bliss among the lotus ponds and golden halls of Amida's Western Paradise.

Genshin's teaching appealed initially to Kyoto's aristocrats. Later Honen (1133–1212) and his disciple Shinran (1173–1262) would popularise Amidism and Nembutsu across all society. The glories of Amida's paradise were first given visual representation in large painted mandalas hung in halls of worship. Later, temples built in partial imitation gave the faithful a tangible idea of the bliss awaiting them in the next world. They included, in their more developed forms, lotus ponds with islands and bridges across which souls would pass entering paradise.

Motsuji at Hiraizumi and Ganjoji at Uchigo near Iwaki are recently reconstructed large paradise gardens in beautiful settings, the latter still possessing its Amida hall. Joruriji, near Nara, presents a smaller, charmingly rural version. Saihoji, the so-called Moss Temple in Kyoto, originally a paradise garden and later a Zen garden, now green and softly lit with dappled light, evokes the most mysterious, unworldly atmosphere of all.

The long and spectacular classical period closed with these gardens, although they and their predecessors would be reinterpreted continually over the forthcoming centuries. Medieval Japan, a time of warrior rule and feudalism, was imminent. New garden types would be introduced in a period that can be seen as the most artistically creative in the nation's cultural history, while the most disturbed politically.

Zen: Essence, Metaphor and Allusion

The three centuries of the Northern Sung Dynasty (960–1126) and Southern Sung Dynasty (1127–1279) were a period of great cultural achievement in China, not the least in painting and garden-making. Long-held fascination with wilderness and the country's jagged mountain ranges found pictorial expression in paintings such as 'Buddhist Temple amid clearing mountain peaks' by tenth-century artist Li Ch'eng, illustrated in Maggie Keswick's book, The Chinese Garden. 'A vast precipice looms over a Buddhist temple; trees with crab-claw branches are perched way out on crags which echo their shape. Below, tiny peasants approach an inn . . .' The inn is partly built over a river flowing from the foot of a towering two-step waterfall that emerges from a high and distant cleavage. The temple, its upswept eaves in tune with spiky trees, sits securely on a middle-level promontory and offers, like the inn below, some sense of human comfort in an otherwise overwhelming terrain.

Period paintings of garden scenes show tall, fissured and pitted rocks. To the imaginative eye they are the soaring mist-veiled peaks illustrated in landscape paintings. Painting and garden-making interacted symbiotically as each sought to encapsulate the dramatic and monumental nature of China's mountain scenery.

The medieval era in Japan's history began with the shift of political power from Kyoto to Kamakura (near Tokyo) where Minamoto no Yoritomo, the first shogun (generalissimo), had established his headquarters. During the Kamakura period (1185–1392), Japanese Buddhist masters returned from study in China with Ch'an Buddhism, or Zen Buddhism as it became known in Japan, a self-reliant teaching then flourishing in monasteries around West Lake in the city of Hangzhou. Its austere discipline found favour with the warrior class and received official patronage. Zen monasteries were founded in Kamakura and Kyoto, where they became centres of Chinese learning and progenitors of a new wave of garden-making.

No firm evidence links Japanese Zen gardens with gardens in Chinese Ch'an temples, but the Zen temple, Kenchoji in Kamakura was modelled after a notable Ch'an Buddhist temple and included a pond garden with an island at the time of its foundation in c 1253. Early Zen temples included pond gardens in the 'contemplation' style, that is, gardens intended to be viewed from within a building. Zen teaching stressed what Joan Stanley-Baker in Japanese Art calls 'the futility of extraneous intellectual and artistic activity', but used poems and ink drawings to demonstrate various aspects of enlightenment. Gardens too may have served as aids to meditation and, ultimately, enlightenment or, as Nitschke suggests, the reverse could be the case: that 'garden architects and their creations were profoundly influenced by the enlightenment and psychological insights gained through meditation'.

The garden at Tenryuji in Kyoto includes rock arrangements distinctly Sung in style. In the pond, towards the shore furthest from the temple, a group of seven rocks form a *horai* island. The rocks have strong vertical emphasis, particularly the climactic, slightly tilted, peak. Behind is a *karedaki* or dry waterfall. Above a large vertical flat-faced rock rising from the water – the lower fall – is a cascade of rocks suggesting rapids; one rock in this assemblage looks like a carp swimming upstream. This is an early example in Japan of a *ryumonbaku*. It represents legendary Ryumon (Dragon Gate) Falls in the Yellow River and is combined with a *rigyoseki*, a stone depicting a carp that, according to legend, would turn into a dragon and enter heaven if it could ascend the falls. In its spatial depth and dramatic rockwork, this waterfall composition recalls a Sung dynasty landscape painting.

Tenryuji's famous *karedaki* and *horai* island.

Saihoji was converted to a Zen temple by Muso Soseki in 1339, and to the old paradise garden an upper-level garden was added for religious training. This includes three rock arrangements that were to become common elements in Zen gardens. The first, or lowest, is a *kamejima* set in moss, not water. Next is a *zazenseki*, a flat meditation stone, and finally there is an exceptionally powerful *karedaki* said by master gardener Yoshikawa Isao to represent a powerful torrent 'purging the world of all pollution'.

A splendid carp stone at Kinkakuji.

Evolution of a native Zen tradition was partly inspired by Sung dynasty paintings imported into Japan as well as by immigrant artists from China. The Muromachi period (1392–1568) marks the shogunate's return to Kyoto, and during its early years Japanese-born Zen painter-priests became skilled in Buddhist art. Sesshu Toyo (1420–1506), the Zen priest regarded as Japan's greatest exponent of ink landscape painting, also made gardens, two of which retain much of their original form today. Joeiji, built at Yamaguchi in western Japan in the late fifteenth century, illustrates the period's painting/garden-making synthesis. Sesshu's painting style was based on a dynamic expression of angularly combined straight lines. Loraine Kuck notes how many of the rocks at Joeiji have abruptly delineated flat tops and straight sides and infers that there 'the interrelationship of the gardens to the painted landscape pictures – of stonework to brushwork – came to a full circle when the strokes of the painters were used to recreate the essentials of natural rocks, and actual rocks were used in gardens to suggest the brush strokes of the painters'.

Men from a class of landless people known as *kawaramono*, riverbank dwellers who survived by doing tasks repulsive to upper social echelons, such as butchery, had for some time carried out the hard physical labour of moving rocks and digging ponds in gardens conceived by nobles, priests and artists. The knowledge they gained led, in the Muromachi period, to the emergence of artisans whose skills earned the respect and admiration of high-placed patrons, and from whose ranks came the first professional garden-makers. Most famous of his time was Zen'ami, whose work on Muromachi estate and temple gardens led to his description as 'the greatest in the world in stone placement'. Ashikaga Yoshimasa, who had employed Zen'ami on previous occasions, engaged the ageing *kawaramono* to undertake preliminary studies for his future villa at Higashiyama (Ginkakuji). Although Zen'ami died aged ninety-seven in 1483, about the time construction started, he remains credited with the garden's design by a number of scholars.

Karesansui or 'withered mountain water' gardens, appeared in the Muromachi period. The technique of substituting raked white gravel for water liberated garden-making from constraints imposed by location, wealth and space, and ushered in the most innovative and imaginative era of garden-making in Japan's history.

Three of Ryoanji's rock groupings.

Ryoanji has the purest extant *karesansui* garden and one of the earliest, built about 1499. Fifteen rocks are arranged in groups of 5–2, 3–2 and 3 in a walled gravel-floored space about the size of a tennis court. A little moss grows around the rocks; there is no other flora although trees can be seen above surrounding walls. The beauty and authority inherent in its composition, its enigmatic nature and its uniqueness have made Ryoanji subject to endless commentary – from explanations of its stone groupings to thoughts on Zen meditation. Analogies to islands in a sea or tiger cubs crossing a river are found unsatisfactory by most writers: there is a sense of something far more profound, mysterious, ineffable. For Loraine Kuck the garden intentionally expresses 'that Harmony which underlies the universe, the world, and man. The Harmony of force and matter and spirit. The Harmony that, to the Oriental religionist, makes the morning stars to sing together, the heart of nature to beat in rhythm, and man to know himself a brother of the rocks and wind and sun.' Ryoanji's garden is, she concludes, 'one the world's great masterpieces of religiously inspired art'.

Daisen-in, built c 1513 in Kyoto, possesses a famous *karesansui* example of what Kuck calls 'painting gardens'. An enclosed L-shaped space, about 4 metres (13 feet) wide, is dominated by a graphic rock composition with towering crags that flank a recessed waterfall and lesser peaks. Below the fall rapids spill into a river that branches and broadens in two directions: west past a *kamejima* and a *kokamejima* (a small turtle island in a garden that already has a larger one) into the 'middle sea', and south under a stone bridge past a *tsurujima* and other rocks to the calm implied sea of the south garden.

Nitschke finds meanings beyond the pictorial at Daisen-in. At one level the garden symbolises the flow of life from effervescent youth (the rapids) through the vicissitudes of middle life, where rocks may represent obstacles or rewards, to the serenity of old age represented by the south garden. At a deeper level, accessible to Zen adepts, 'the rocks become the difficulties encountered in the search for the answer to that most fundamental of *koan* – Who am I?'

The southern garden to the *hojo* at Juko-in, a sub-temple of Daitokuji, is one of few Momoyama-period (1568–1615) temple gardens open to the public, and then only at special periods during winter months. A moss-covered rectangular space is backed by a trimmed hedge said to represent mountains. Running across the garden in front of the hedge a chain of small rocks – islands – are arranged in two groups connected by a stone bridge in a composition with a striking resemblance to the lower part of a painting by Bunsei known as *West Lake*, thought to be painted in the 1460s and illustrated in *Japanese Art*. It too shows a bridge connecting two rock-strewn islands, the background fading away over a misty lake to distant hills. We see in both the painting and the garden a horizontal emphasis, hinting at Japanese landscape rather than the steepness portrayed in Sung art and seen at Daisen-in. While no direct link between Bunsei's painting and Juko-in's garden can be inferred, taken together they illustrate the sustained cross-fertilisation between the two art forms as the Japanese continued to adapt the imported culture to indigenous circumstances.

Daisen-in

Fine Zen gardens continued to be built in the Edo period (1615–1867) but the creative energies that drove the Muromachi and Momoyama periods were beginning to subside. Gardens tended to be in stereotypical pond or *karesansui* styles. Pond gardens were often built against hillsides, with ponds close to *shoin* (writing halls) or Buddha halls serving as reservoirs in case of fire. *Karesansui* gardens such as Manshu-in suggest natural scenery in the forms of islands and lakes, while Nanzenji Hojo continues the tradition of abstract composition, if with a tendency to naturalism in the arrangement of rocks and plants. Three gardens, the *o-karikomi*, or topiary gardens at Raikyuji in Takahashi, Konchi-in in Kyoto, and Daichiji in Minakuchi, stand out from the stereotypes. All are attributed to one of Japan's greatest garden designers, Kobori Enshu (1579–1647), or his pupils.

Hitherto, symbols in gardens had been created with rocks, plants having secondary roles. In these three gardens bushes are massed and clipped to become major forms and, in the cases of Raikyuji and Daichiji, significant symbolic statements. At Raikyuji, built between 1604 and 1619, azaleas at the back of the garden are shaped to represent towering, billowing waves. Another *o-karikomi* formation surrounds a triadic rock group – perhaps here the plant forms represent waves crashing against an island. The hillside bushes at Konchi-in, built in 1632, are rounded – perhaps suggesting mountain ranges – and the crane and turtle islands have graphic rock formations, but at Daichiji, built in the mid-seventeenth century, the hedge provides the dominant symbol. A sinuous azalea coil said to represent a treasure ship occupies mid-stage; other hedges outline waves, another a turtle island. There are very few rocks.

Raikyuji's great wave sculptured hedge.

While Daichiji may manifest a transmutation of roles between rocks and plants in a highly evolved form, a decline in the importance of rocks and a heightened interest in topiary is characteristic of the Edo period. At Shodenji, a quiet Zen temple in the outskirts of Kyoto, there is a small walled *karesansui* garden where the only embellishments are clipped azalea bushes arranged in 3-5-7 groups, just as the rocks are in Ryoanji. Shodenji conclusively represents the liberation from locational and economic restraints afforded by *karesansui*; even the costs of acquiring and placing rocks could be avoided. A garden could be made with the simplest of means anywhere.

The Significance of Rocks

Triads are among the most potent archetypes in human culture. Christian theology, for example, centres on the Holy Trinity and stands three crosses on Calvary at its climactic moment. Triadic compositions are the most pervasive of all rock groups in Japanese gardens, where they often symbolise Buddha with two attendant *bodhisattvas* (Buddhist saints who have postponed their own Nirvana).

Three-rock settings were probably commonplace in classical gardens. The *Sakuteiki*, the garden treatise written during the Heian period, describes Horizontal Triad Rocks, *hinbonseki*, and Buddhist Triad Rocks, *sanzonseki*. The former is a group of three rocks disposed on a horizontal plane in a triangular formation resembling the Chinese character for articles, *hin*. The latter arranges three rocks as a triangle in the vertical plane; a central, taller rock is flanked by two lower rocks in a manner that recalls symbolically Buddhist triads found in temple statuary, yet advances aesthetically from iconographic symmetry. The uneven height of the two supporting rocks – one low, one of medium height – brings into play universal and timeless questions of balance and proportion. Günter Nitschke observes that 'a dynamic balance of odd numbers is not merely limited to garden architecture, but lies at the heart of Noh theatre and the art of flower arrangement (*ikebana*)'. The three basic components in an *ikebana* arrangement are a tall 'branch of truth', or *ten* (heaven), a low lateral stem symbolising *chi* (earth), and between them an inclined stem symbolising *jin* (man). Aesthetic balance in this context may be said to represent the ideal harmony desirable under the cosmological principle that heaven, earth and man constantly interact in all aspects of existence.

A later text, *Illustrations for Designing Mountain, Water and Hillside Field Landscapes*, published in 1466 and translated in David A. Slawson's *Secret Teachings in the Art of Japanese Gardens*, illustrates that symbolism attached to rock formations had become more complex by the Muromachi period, with an amplification of two themes: the naming of rocks and the cosmic laws governing their selection and placement.

This text refers to the naming of forty-eight rocks in Japan, fewer than the Chinese count of three hundred and sixty-one, but rather more than the average garden viewer may wish to identify. Slawson enthusiastically discusses their relationship to scenic, sensory or cultural values and geological zones, and the rules governing selection and assemblage. This is far too complex a subject to cover here, but Slawson's translation of *Illustrations* indicates the poetic nature of the process and the careful search necessary to find the most desirable rock for its setting, involving for instance the precise selection of a rock's grain and its dynamic use to express the disposition of the three forces, horizontal, diagonal and vertical, equivalent to the triad of Heaven, Earth and Man. Certain major rocks were also cited as a determining factor, needing selection and placement before allocation of subsidiaries, notably the Rock of the Spirit Kings and the one representing Mt Horai (the Never Aging Rock), with its accompanying Rock of Ten Thousand Eons depicting the ancient turtle of Horai.

Rock triad at Ryutanji, Kiga.

Slawson says these rocks refer to the cultural aspect, while others with equally evocative names – Hovering Mist Rock, Dragon's Abode Rocks, Frolicking Birds Rocks – relate to scenic effects, and rocks such as the Rock of Perfect Beauty and Crescent Configuration Rocks convey sensory impressions. While such names, occasionally mentioned in temple pamphlets and other 'popular' writings, ascribe meaning and distinction to otherwise similar natural objects, the names of lesser rocks are relatively esoteric and unnecessary for general enjoyment or understanding of gardens.

Shakkei, or Borrowed Scenery

> *I built my hut in a zone of human habitation,*
> *Yet near me there sounds no noise*
> *of horse or coach.*
> *Would you know how that is possible?*
>
> *A heart that is distant*
> *creates a wilderness around it.*
> *I pluck chrysanthemums*
> *under the eastern hedge,*
> *Then gaze long*
> *at the distant southern hills.*

Chinese poet T'ao Ch'ien (378–427)

Thought to be the earliest example of *shakkei*, hazy mountains echo the closer tree line at Tenryuji on a spring morning.

Chinese gardens have included beautiful distant scenery since at least the third century AD, when nature-lovers built small pavilions in natural sites to capture certain views, effectively transforming landscapes into gardens. Japanese gardens also have included scenes beyond their boundaries since Heian times, yet the term *shakkei* did not appear in Japan until the nineteenth century. This followed publication in China in the early seventeenth century of *Yuan-yeh*, a garden-making treatise that included a chapter on *chieh-ching* (techniques for including borrowed landscapes in garden design), and was in line with a more academic approach taken to garden design in the Meiji period. The Japanese term for bringing remote features, such as mountains, into garden design was originally *ikedori*, or 'capturing alive', implying both possession – the remote scene becomes part of the garden – and symbiosis, as the nearby and the distant add life to each other.

In *Space and Illusion in the Japanese Garden* Itoh Teiji draws attention to techniques that characterise *shakkei* gardens and distinguish them from being merely gardens with views. The first is *mikiri* or 'trimming'. Structures, embankments or plantings are arranged to eliminate irrelevant parts of borrowed scenery and to emphasise desirable aspects. The second is linking, or layering, where the middle ground in a composition is modulated or articulated to draw foreground and background together.

At Tenryuji, the earliest extant example of a *shakkei* garden, tree heights beyond the pond are controlled so that the profile of Arashiyama is furthermost in a series of layered planes.

The garden at Entsuji, in the northern foothills of Kyoto, 'captures' distant Mt Hiei through brilliant manipulation of middle-ground elements. East of the temple is a moss-covered rectangle about 560 square metres (670 square yards) in area. Featuring a number of rock arrangements, this mossy area is bordered on three unenclosed sides by a clipped hedge about 1.2 metres (4 feet) high. A bamboo grove outside the garden is trimmed to look like a feathery upper layer of the hedge. Mt Hiei is seen above these bamboos, framed in a space completed by the linked foliage of cryptomeria and cypress trees. The peak of Mt Hiei is not central in the overall composition but to one side; balance is restored by massing larger rock groups towards the other side of the garden.

The middle ground at Entsuji also links elements in the landscape with the temple's architecture. Repetitive tree trunks echo posts; the vertical and horizontal planes of the clipped hedge repeat the lines of floors, walls and eaves. In this way, in a remarkable synthesis, Entsuji's composition unites the building you are in with a landscape element over 6 kilometres (about 4 miles) away.

Another outstanding example of *shakkei* is Shugakuin in the eastern hills of Kyoto, where the design of the upper garden borrows the western ranges and the valley in which the city is built, with the overarching sky as unifying factor. At Isuien in Nara the roof of the Great South Gate to Todaiji, although vast, appears to hover on the edge of the garden like a tea house by virtue of distance-reduced scale and intervening trees. Urban development has compromised many old examples of *shakkei* – indeed, Entsuji was fighting a proposal for a tall hotel in the middle of its famous composition when we were there in 1992 – but in the remote hill town of Chiran, southern Kyushu, you can see samurai houses where distant hills are as much parts of gardens now as they were centuries ago.

Dewy Paths

Tea had already been long valued in China for medicinal qualities when its cultivation was introduced to Japan in the late twelfth century. With the advent of Zen Buddhism, priests found its stimulating qualities helpful in staying awake during long periods of meditation, as had their predecessors in Chinese monasteries. Rituals and social practices that evolved from the consumption of tea became an integral part of Zen culture. These practices became codified in the tea ceremony and absorbed into secular culture. Designers and makers of buildings and gardens associated with the tea ceremony eventually adopted an aesthetic of simplicity and artful casualness, attitudes originating in the idealised virtues of rural frugality expressed in an ambience of cultivated refinement.

A roji at Yushintei, Sento Gosho.

The spiritual essence of *cha-no-yu*, the tea ceremony, is contained in four principles: *wa*, harmony between man, nature and the universe; *kei*, personal humility and respect for others; *sei*, cleanliness and order in all things; and *jaku*, cultivation of serenity and repose. The *roji*, passageway or dewy path, was the avenue through which one could shed the contaminating preoccupations of daily life and approach the spiritual receptiveness necessary to participate in the ceremony itself. This transition – emotionally from one state to another, physically from an entry gate to a tea house – introduced a new garden type that would influence the next and last great garden style, the stroll gardens of the Edo period.

The traditional *roji* is divided into two parts, an outer section where arriving guests might wait for one another, and an inner section leading to the tea house. It is contrived to appear natural, to suggest, in the words of Itoh Teiji, a path through some 'remote mysterious valley' and arranged to provide the passer-through with a sequence of beautifully crafted but seemingly accidental incidents. Informally disposed small stepping stones control movement and concentrate attention. A larger mid-journey stone invites a pause, a raising of the eyes, and awareness of some special vista or detail. Objects such as lanterns, used in gardens for the first time, and water basins for ritual purification are preferred in natural materials, old and weathered. Things discarded or abandoned – votive lanterns from ruined temples, millstones, rural pottery, imperfect tea bowls – have places both in the garden and within the elegant rustication of the tea house, but only when selected by a discerning eye. The character required in artefacts is expressed by the terms *wabi*, loosely translated as more in less, and *sabi*, or patina, an elegance induced by time alone.

Within the tea house, concentration is on the ceremony itself: the garden may be barely visible. Its role is to provide a setting for a journey from the complexity and uncertainty of the world at large to tea house simplicity and tranquillity. The open interrelationship between a Zen temple interior and its contemplated garden has been inverted, setting the stage for a new development where a journey, extended and freed of metaphysical overtones, becomes the major theme around which entire gardens are designed.

Momoyama Opulence

The late Muromachi period was a time of civil warfare and widespread destruction, beginning with the Onin War (1467–1477) which devastated Kyoto and continuing as a power struggle among feudal lords until supremacy and order was ruthlessly established by Oda Nobunaga in 1568. Stability was consolidated under Toyotomi Hideyoshi and secured for the long term by Tokugawa Ieyasu when he established the Tokugawa shogunate in Edo (present-day Tokyo) in 1603. The years between 1568 and 1615 are known as the Momoyama period, named after the location of the castle Hideyoshi built near Kyoto. They are also a time of transition, as Japan moved from a medieval society to one historians define as pre-modern.

Historian Conrad Totman characterises the period's culture as marked by 'creative braggadocio' as rulers and warlords worked to conceal plebeian origins by mastering the refined sensibilities of Kyoto culture. Buildings and gardens reflected the arrogance of their owners within an ambience of refined magniloquence. Both Nobunaga and Hideyoshi employed Sen no Rikyu, the great tea master who established the principles of ritual and deportment known as Sado (the Way of Tea), for their tea ceremonies but Hideyoshi built tea houses in two styles – one an expression of frugality to show himself a man of taste, the other coated in gold to demonstrate his wealth.

Daimyo (provincial lords) displayed their wealth and indulged their creativity by collecting impressively large rocks and having them assembled in compositions that Nitschke describes as 'simpler than their predecessors, and at the same time more powerful, energetic and three dimensional'. The garden now known as Senshukaku Teien, built c 1590 as the garden to Tokushima Castle, Shikoku, exemplifies this vigorous approach. Large striated and smaller smooth rocks are strewn, as if by glacial deposit, across interconnecting pond and dry gardens with a sense of dissipated brute force. A massive two-piece stone bridge linking the crane and turtle islands in the dry garden is over 10 metres (34 feet) long, probably the longest in Japan.

Sambo-in, just south of Kyoto, is regarded as the most representative garden of the period. In 1598 Hideyoshi elected to redesign an existing garden for a cherry blossom-viewing party. Three hundred workers were engaged in placing some seven hundred rocks acquired by purchase, command or plunder and planting innumerable rare trees over an area of about 0.5 hectare (1.25 acres). The pond and island design can now be viewed only from verandahs, but this is not a garden for contemplation; its superabundance of material and incident creates a visual restlessness that leads the eye from one picturesque composition to another. Sambo-in, flamboyant reminder of Momoyama exhibitionism, presages in its dynamic irresolution the stroll gardens of the Edo period.

Unfolding Pleasures

The Katsura Imperial Villa, built in Kyoto between 1615 and 1645, is renowned as the quintessential expression of Japanese architecture and garden-making, its reputation elevated to the iconic heights of Versailles and the Taj Mahal but its form and structure the very antithesis of such monumentality. The designers and builders of Katsura applied the understated delicacy of the tea house and the spatial progression of the *roji* to the scale of a princely estate. The result was a mansion of spare, relaxed elegance and a garden of exquisite informality designed to be enjoyed either as framed compositions from within the perfect pavilions or as a presentation of vistas encountered on a walk around the large free-form pond.

Late autumn at Sento Gosho.

The garden at Sento Gosho, principle residence of retired Emperor Gomizuno-o, was built to the design of Kobori Enshu between 1634 and 1636. Gomizuno-o built his rural retreat, Shugakuin, over several levels on the slopes of Kyoto's eastern mountains between 1655 and 1659. Both these imperial estates exploited the spatial dynamics created for Katsura and the three established the style that would become known as 'stroll garden'. This style of garden would be adopted for vast estates built in the new capital, Edo, and also in the provinces.

The stroll gardens of the Edo period (1615–1867) can be likened to music for the way in which rhythms, variations, developments and recapitulations are perceived over time. The basic components – ponds, islands, artificial mountains, planting, open spaces, watercourses, tea houses, employment of *shakkei* and allusions to famous places – are

Suizenji Park at Kumamoto.

derived from established traditions. New is the way in which paths and the components themselves are manipulated to conceal or expose various parts sequentially in a technique known as 'hide and reveal'. This concept embodies progress in space and time, contrast and surprise, as in movement from contained space to open, from shadowy gloom to bright light, from waterside vista to elevated panorama. Stepping stones might demand attention, a forest glade might enclose, a hedge or mound might obstruct: intermissions in an unfolding drama that stages one fascinating scene after another.

The Tokugawa regime based in Edo consolidated its own authority and national stability by shackling potential challengers. Daimyo were required to spend every alternate year in the capital. When they returned to their provincial seats their families stayed behind as virtual hostages, and they were obliged to build resource-consuming palaces and gardens. Few of the great Edo gardens that the English architect Josiah Conder described and illustrated with photographs in his book *Landscape Gardening in Japan* (published in 1893) remain and then sometimes only in depleted forms – Tokyo's Korakuen today is only a little more than a quarter of its former size. Better-preserved generally are gardens built by daimyo in their feudal seats. Korakuen in Okayama, Kenrokuen in Kanazawa, and Ritsurin Park in Takamatsu are outstanding examples now open to the public.

These latterday stroll gardens, often built over long periods by successive generations, might be described as the travel documentaries of their time. Their theme is famous sights, either as referred to in literature or actually seen. Representations of these sights are organised sequentially using hide and reveal techniques. They may be only vaguely allusive, or alternatively appear as realistic miniatures, as in the Mt Fuji mound at Suizenji Park, Kumamoto. Walking around Korakuen in Tokyo you see, among other scenic splendours, the slopes of Lu-shan (a mountain in the north of Jiangxi province in China), the view from the terrace at Kiyomizu at Kyoto and the peaks and gorges of Kiso in Nagano prefecture. Rural life is represented in a small rice field. Sets of garden prospects were often built around favoured numbers, as in the 'Eight Famous Views of Omi', referring to fancied scenery around Lake Biwa and noted in Shimizuen in Shibata. Rikugien, begun in 1695, restored in 1877 and best-preserved of the Tokyo gardens, professes eighty-eight scenic sites, all with literary connections to classical China or Japan.

The Modern Era

Two hundred years of isolation imposed on Japan by the Tokugawa shoguns ended when a friendship treaty with the United States of America was signed in 1854, and by 1868 the shogunate had been overthrown and imperial rule restored. The nation began assimilating western culture and technologies as quickly as possible, neglecting, or at worst abandoning, many of its own traditions in the process. In a cultural environment that must have been both heady with liberation from old prescriptive practices and confusing, two new main styles of art emerged. One was *yoga*, the Japanese name for western oil painting, and the other *nihonga*, in which traditional styles were sustained but modified with such western-style techniques as chiaroscuro and brighter colours. At its best, *nihonga* produced some of the loveliest, most lyrical, paintings in the history of Japanese art. In similar vein, one Meiji period (1868–1912) garden in Kyoto welds traditional details to a naturalistic theme that echoes, in a beautiful and original synthesis, contemporary western artists' absorption in natural landscapes.

Late autumn at Murin-an.

Ogawa Jihei, the period's leading landscape designer, built Murin-an in 1896 for Yamagata Aritomo, an important Meiji period statesman. At first glance, Murin-an looks like some small alpine meadow fringed with trees and dotted, in late spring, with tiny blue flowers. Closer inspection reveals a sophisticated composition of pools and streams coursing, with exquisite variation in pitch and dynamism, through and around undulating grassy swards furnished with rocks and low clipped bushes. In a typical example of *shakkei*, the screen of trees is notched out at the apex of the garden's triangular shape to capture a view of nearby Higashiyama (Eastern Mountains). While this garden offers no levels of experience beyond the sensory, its execution is steeped in centuries-old skills and artistry.

Although other excellent gardens were built during the Meiji period, none open to the public convey the freshness of vision seen at Murin-an. The Heian Shrine's garden in Kyoto, also by Ogawa, is necessarily eclectic in its recapitulation of the Heian period. Isuien in Nara is charming in a traditional way and includes a fine example of *shakkei*. In Tokyo, Iwasaki Yataro, founder of the Mitsubishi Company, renovated Rikugien and built Kiyosumi Garden in the manner of an Edo-period stroll garden.

During the Showa period (1926–1989) modernism became the dominant architectural style worldwide, particularly in the stripped-down form known as the International Style which rejected history, context and decoration for an aesthetic governed by functional requirements and technology. Although the style originated in Europe and evolved in America it owed some of its ideology to the modular system of construction based on a tatami mat and to the spare *sukiya* style of architecture exemplified at Katsura and publicised by the modernist pioneer architect Bruno Taut. Garden design in Japan underwent a parallel movement away from naturalism towards abstraction, again with traditional antecedents. Ryoanji's rock garden looks remarkably modern to eyes familiar with mid to late twentieth-century abstract art.

An abstraction of checkerboard paving nestles in moss at Tofukuji's north garden.

A modern 'winding stream' at Shonandai Cultural Centre.

Ando's Garden of Fine Art.

The scholar, historian and garden designer Shigemori Mirei, who studied at the National Art Academy, designed four gardens at the Hojo in Tofukuji in 1938. The south garden has a traditional feeling in the way it uses rocks, raked sand and moss mounds. Gardens on the west and north depart radically into abstract compositions based on alternating squares of stone and plant materials, while the east garden reflects time-honoured interest in cosmology with a representation of the Great Bear constellation that uses old foundation stones.

Among those who have designed important gardens in the post-war period are the Japanese-American sculptor Isamu Noguchi and Tange Kenzo, designer of the building and forecourt for the Prefectural Offices at Takamatsu where quarried rather than natural rocks are used. More recently Ando Tadao has created the dazzling oval pond through which you descend to the main hall at Honpukuji on Awaji Island.

While the gardens mentioned above are 'modern' with their emphasis on abstraction and, in some cases, geometrical shapes, they all use either traditional materials or plant life. Some recent projects move further away from common expectations and raise questions about the very meaning of the word 'garden'. At the Shonandai Cultural Centre in Fujisawa, architect Hasegawa Itsuko inverts the trend to abstraction in her synthetic reinterpretation of a winding stream, one of the oldest garden archetypes. Using only industrial materials, this garden of metallic trees and a tiled waterway acts as a play-space for the adjacent children's library, a function far removed from the exclusive atmosphere of its aristocratic antecedents. The Garden of Fine Art in Kyoto, an open-roof concrete enclosure designed by Ando, borrows occasional framed views of the adjacent Botanic Gardens as its only gesture to naturalism. Within are walls streaming with water, ponds, and galleries on several levels designed as positions for admiring 'famous views' – ceramic reproductions of famous eastern and western art masterpieces. Like sand planes in *karesansui* gardens, the ponds separate people from the 'art works', while the sequencing of positions that define the viewer/object relationship gives a spatial organisation similar to a multi-level stroll garden.

It is ironic that while western enthusiasm for Japanese gardens extends to mere duplication of a charm school vision of prettiness, Japanese garden designers continue to advance into new territories, where the limitation of working from tradition seems only to provide a springboard to new invention. However, in itself, this is consistent with a past of continuing innovation and daring experiment.

3

GARDENS EAST AND
NORTH OF KYOTO

Motsuji

Hiraizumi • Iwate Prefecture • Heian Period

. . . .

Peaceful survivors from Heian glory, a majestic turtle island in a lake surrounded by pebble shores.

The Oizumi Pond at Motsuji, lying peacefully among ancient cryptomerias and wooded hills, was once the centrepiece of a great paradise garden built by Fujiwara lords in the twelfth century, when Hiraizumi was a flourishing northern satellite of classical culture.

While shores and the central *horai* island are recent reconstructions, several major rock groups have survived from the Heian period. These include a *kamejima* whose tall headstone dramatically counterpoints horizontal shorelines and forms the pond's focal point, a nearby peninsula and a *tsukiyama* (artificial mountain) in the south-west corner. A beautiful reconstructed winding stream enters from the north-east.

Present buildings bear no relation to the vermilion temples, halls, towers, bridges and gate that graced the original garden, but traditional festivals are held in winter (20 Jan), spring (1–5 May) and autumn (1–3 Nov) to recapture the rituals and colours of former times. A 'Floating Poetry Festival' takes place along the banks of the winding stream on the fourth Sunday each May. The garden has been designated Special Historical Remains (1952) and Special Scenic Spot (1959) for its archaeological importance and spectacular beauty.

E1 *Motsuji is about 10 minutes' walk from Hiraizumi station along the road at right angles to the tracks. A visit to Motsuji can easily be combined with one to Chusonji, where the jewel-like Konjikido (Golden Hall), a National Treasure, is preserved in an encasing building. (See map E1)*

Domon Ken Kinenkan

Sakata • Yamagata Prefecture • Showa Period

The Domon Ken Kinenkan (Memorial Hall) houses and displays varying selections from the work of this famous Sakata-born photographer. Located on the edge of a small lake in the Mount Iimori Culture Park, the fine modern building is complemented by two spare and elegant gardens, both carefully integrated with interior spaces, yet connecting fluently with landscapes beyond.

On the lake frontage, a courtyard of water-flooded stone terraces features a sculptured standing rock suggestive of a modern Mt Horai

Noguchi's sculpture stands among sparkling ripples splashing over shallow stone terraces in this lakeside courtyard.

interpretation, donated by the Japanese-American sculptor Isamu Noguchi. While this bright courtyard can be entered, views into it are framed by a series of windows off a corridor; a relationship between structural mass and water that echoes the broader-scale connection between the building and the lake.

The *karesansui* garden, at the end of a further gallery, is seen through a wide window-wall. A row of chairs invites contemplation of a sloping field of white pebbles with mounds of spiky bamboo grass rising to merge with a low hillside.

E2 *The Hall is about 15 minutes' bus ride from the right-hand side stop in front of the Sakata station (bus bound for Ii-Moriyama Bunka Koen). Alight at the Domon Ken Kinenkan-mae stop. Closed Mondays.*

Homma Bijutsukan

Sakata • Yamagata Prefecture • Edo Period

· ·

The garden of the Homma Bijutsukan (Art Museum), known as Tsurumaien, was built in 1813 as an aid to relieve unemployment. It was attached to the Homma family residence which still stands in an elevated corner. Lushly planted, it is a picturesque and compact stroll garden around a small irregularly formed pond. There is an island in the pond, an artificial mountain and a rich array of details including a tea house, lanterns, a stone pagoda and timber bridges in two types of construction – one with offset planks to compel a midstream pause.

While Tsurumaien may conform to a stereotypical genre, it is undeniably attractive, carefully maintained and more than likely to be peaceful at any time.

E3 *The Homma Art Museum is near the Sakata station. Turn right on the road opposite the main entrance, walk along past the Hotel Alpha One; the gallery is on the first major intersection. Entrance to the garden is included with museum admission. Closed Mondays.*

A maze of flowers, rounded bushes, paths and small garden structures makes the Homma garden a delightful diversion.

Gyokusenji

Haguro • Yamagata Prefecture • Edo Period

A lantern stands among irises. Primulas, the temple's flower emblem, is a pervading spring counterpoint to the more formal bushes.

Gyokusenji is located in a peaceful foothills village among rice fields on the edge of the Shonai Plain. The temple is said to date from the Kamakura period; the present garden was built in the early Edo period with foreground stepping stones added in the Meiji period. Gyokusenji's special charm lies in the garden's beauty, its friendly atmosphere and the way visitors are permitted to wander through rooms and garden, seeing each from many vantage points.

The garden is set between the temple and a steep hillside. The pond contains three islands. Banks and islands are connected with stone slab bridges and decorated with clipped azalea bushes, lanterns and angular, strongly scaled rocks. To the right-hand, rear side there is a rock waterfall, partly overgrown. Interspersed with lower plants are small evergreen trees, carefully pruned to provide vertical transitional forms between the rounded azaleas and hillside vegetation, so tying the manicured pond area to its natural setting.

E4 *Take the Hagurosan bus from in front of Tsuruoka Station. Alight after about 15 minutes just before the large red torii across the main road; a small road off to the right will take you past rice fields to a small cluster of houses. The temple is just around to the left.*

In one of the prettiest late-spring gardens, a riot of cascading azaleas drapes down the hill face above Gyokusenji's pond.

Shimizuen

Shibata • Niigata Prefecture • Edo Period

A memory of Katsura re-enacted in a provincial setting, an intimate lantern stands, in late sunlight, at the end of a pebbled peninsula in Shimizuen's pond.

Shimizuen was once the garden of a Sotoshu Sect Buddhist temple. The Tokugawa shogunate appropriated the land in 1658, the temple moved to a neighbouring district, and feudal lord Mizoguchi Hidekatsu completed a residence on the site in 1666. The beautiful recently restored garden was completed about 1700 by Mizoguchi Shigekatsu assisted by Agata Sochi, a tea master of the Enshu style and gardener to the shogunate.

Shimizuen is laid out as a stroll garden around a large pond shaped after the water ideogram and designed to present the 'Eight Famous Views of Omi', a reference to beautiful scenery around Lake Biwa in the province of Omi (present-day Shiga prefecture). Meandering along shady banks, the path around the pond reveals many lovely scenes, prominently among them a pebbled peninsula with a lantern at its tip in an arrangement rather similar to the famous one at Katsura Imperial Villa in Kyoto. Tea rooms are located at strategic points. One known as Yukatei overhangs the pond to provide a focal point to many vistas, while a bridge made of massive, staggered granite blocks forms the garden's most striking artefact.

E5 *Shibata is an old castle town about 30 kilometres (20 miles) north-east of Niigata on the JR Hakushin line. Shimizuen is a short walk from the station. Closed 26 Dec–5 Jan. (See map E5)*

Ganjoji

Uchigo • Fukushima Prefecture • Heian period

. . . .

The Amida hall of Ganjoji, built in 1160, is one of few surviving Heian structures and a National Treasure. The weathered three-bay square building with a pyramid shingle roof overlooks a broad enwrapping pond within an arc of luxuriantly wooded hills.

Restoration work on the garden has been under way since 1966, when the 18.5 hectare (46 acre) site was declared a National Historic Place. Bridges linking the entrance gate to the central island, and the island to the hall, were being reconstructed in 1995. The completed pond is elegantly detailed with pebbled shores showing occasional rock groups, some small rocky islands, and is in places fringed with irises. With such a beautiful setting, the work being carried out should see Ganjoji's paradise garden re-emerge into one of the most captivating in Japan.

Ganjoji's Amida hall and pond sit in a natural amphitheatre of wooded hills; a site of special presence.

E6 *Uchigo is a few minutes by train from Iwaki station on a local JR line. The temple is an easy 30-minute walk from the station, where an old painted map shows the route via the busy major road fairly well. A more pleasant alternative is to cross the railway line earlier, over a blue-painted pedestrian bridge; walk through a short lane, over the next road and cross the river via a wooden bridge. Straight ahead, slightly left, a narrow street runs in the same direction. Sighting on the distant temple roofs (not Ganjoji, it is to the right), you can stroll up through small streets. If you hit the river further up, follow that and ask when you get close to the hills. We came back this way. There is also a bus along the main road.*

Kairakuen

Mito • Ibaraki Prefecture • Edo Period

樂園

Windy grey dusty weather made photographs dull; the entrance map gives a better feeling for the garden's ambitious scope and varied planning.

Kairakuen's puzzling status as one of the trinity of great Japanese gardens along with Korakuen in Okayama and Kenrokuen in Kanazawa may have more to do with sentiment than present-day reality in which railway, highway and urban expansion disrupt its borrowed scenery of river and rural land. Kairakuen, now a pleasant public park with fine cedar and bamboo plantations, is remarkable mainly for a large orchard of *ume* (plum) trees, which must look spectacular when in bloom from late winter to early spring.

Tokugawa Nariaki, ninth son of the Mito clan of the Tokugawa family, created the orchard which was noted for supplying plums to the shogunate's forces and made it into a public park in 1840. A two-storey pavilion, known as Kobuntei, commands expansive views over adjacent lawns and plantations, Lake Semba nearby and distant countryside from its upper floor.

E7 *From Mito station on the Joban Line Kairakuen is 12 minutes' bus ride to Kairakuen-mae bus stop, or about a 30-minute walk through attractive Semba park. Take the main road left in front of the station, the lakeside park soon appears on the left; Kairakuen is on the hill to the right of the far end of the lake.*

Noninji

Hanno • Saitama Prefecture • Edo Period

Noninji's lovely garden was probably built early in the eighteenth century, two centuries after the temple's origins as a small hermitage. It rises up a fairly steep hillside above a narrow pond that spreads towards the main hall from a *karedaki*. A superb clipped hedge arches over the hillside, distinguishing the garden from a frame of trees, and slopes below are modelled into hillocks and valleys studded with miniaturised trees, clipped bushes and rocks, all suggesting mountain scenery. A cave near the *karedaki* adds pictorial depth to the pond and interest to the right-hand side of the scheme, while a *kamejima* in the left-hand side raises an expressive head towards the nearby hall. Noninji was so quiet while we were there, we wonder if visits are usually allowed.

E8 *Hanno is on the Seibu line, departing from Ikebukuro in Tokyo. Walking from the Hanno station to Noninji takes about half an hour.*

Noninji's pond

GARDENS IN TOKYO

E9–E16

The classic view from Fujishiro-toge at Rikugien.

Between 1856 and 1858 Hiroshige immortalised Edo in woodblock prints as a landscape with villages. The city then housed over a million inhabitants, half of them the families, samurai or retainers of daimyo whose estates occupied seventy per cent of the land and must have contributed to the semi-rural nature of its suburbs.

Some thirty-five years later, Josiah Conder recorded daimyo estate gardens of staggering scale and embellishment, such as Toyama-en, built for the daimyo of Owari (in present-day Aichi prefecture), covering 120 acres (about 48.5 hectares) and displaying twenty-five 'remarkable features'. The general destruction of these gardens was under way as a mercantile society began to transform Tokyo into today's megalopolis. In pot plants, window boxes and little office forecourts, rivulets of nature now seep through this mesh of steel and concrete, to coalesce occasionally in public parks and a few gardens that manage to sustain a sense of separate place. Two that we note here are of seasonal interest. Of the others, Rikugien can stand in comparison with great provincial daimyo gardens such as Korakuen in Okayama and Ritsurin Park in Takamatsu.

Rikugien

Tokyo • Edo Period

. . . .

Yanagisawa Yoshiyasu, who rose from son of government official to wealthy daimyo as confidante to fifth shogun Tsunayoshi, created Rikugien over seven years from 1695. The garden deteriorated between his death in 1714 and 1877 when Iwasaki Yataro, founder of the company Mitsubishi, acquired it and undertook renovations. Iwasaki Hisaya donated Rikugien to the City of Tokyo in 1938.

Azaleas shatter monochromatic restraint at Rikugien.

Yanagisawa's literary interests, which he shared with the shogun, are reflected in his garden's name; the *rikugi* being six principles of *waka* (Japanese classical poetry) identified in an ancient Chinese anthology called *The Book of Songs*. Rikugien is said to possess eighty-eight sites with connections to classical Chinese and Japanese literature. A good account of the garden can be seen in Paul Waley's excellent book, *Tokyo Now and Then, an Explorer's Guide*; the English language visitor's guide offered at entry is not particularly enlightening.

Rikugien's meandering route leads around a large pond with a wooded island and a sea-eroded *horaijima* (isle of the immortals), engaging on its way scenes typical of great stroll gardens: sweeps of water, rustic bridges, streams, forest glades, tea houses and restful arbors. From the summit of an artificial mountain called Fujishiro-toge you gaze over an immaculate and beautifully composed panorama, the finest garden prospect in the city.

E9 *Rikugien is in a quiet residential area a short walk from Komagome station on the Yamanote line.*

Korakuen

Tokyo • Edo Period

Tokudaiji-seki

Tokugawa Yorifusa, daimyo of Mito, began construction of Korakuen in 1629 with designer Tokudaiji Sahyoe. After Yorifusa's death his son, Mitsukuni, completed the garden with the assistance of Zhu Shunshui, a refugee Chinese scholar who is thought to have suggested the garden's name, which refers to an old Chinese saying 'the lord must bear sorrow before the people, take pleasure after them'. Although Korakuen was the most famous and best preserved garden in Tokyo at the end of the nineteenth century, now only a quarter of the original 25.5 hectares (63 acres) remains squeezed between the bulbous Tokyo Dome and office towers including Toyota's headquarters, for which it serves as borrowed scenery.

Korakuen combines many famous scenes from China and Japan around a lake with a large, wooded *horai* island. A huge squarish rock standing in water at the island's edge, and known as the Tokudaiji-seki, represents a turtle's head although vertical striations and mature landscaping imply a waterfall. A circuit around the lake takes in scenes such as Lu-shan, a mountain in Jiangxi province represented by a mound covered in bamboo grass, Tsuten-kyo (a maple-viewing bridge in Tofukiji in Kyoto), Engetsu-kyo (a Chinese-style stone bridge), a shrine, a sake house, waterfalls, streams, tree groves, rice fields, iris beds, wisteria trellises and many others. All major features are identified in a map handed out on admission.

E10 *Korakuen is not far from the Korakuen station on the Marunouchi Line.*

Hama Rikyu Garden

Tokyo • Edo Period

. . . .

Hama Rikyu Garden lies on reclaimed marshland, once a hawking reserve presented by the fourth shogun, Tokugawa Ietsuna, to his younger brother Tsunashige for a residential estate. Tsunashige's son, Ienobu, was appointed shogun in 1709. He added pavilions, improved the garden, named the estate Hama Goten (Palace on the Coast) and used it as a summer resort until its

Bridges over the tidal pond link its shores to the island site of tea pavilion Ochaya.

fiery destruction in 1725. Shogun Ienari remodelled the garden at the end of the eighteenth century; a later account describes a picturesque stroll garden with hills, ponds, groves of trees, many pavilions and simulations of coastal scenes. The estate was transferred to the imperial household after the Meiji Restoration in 1868, renamed Hama Rikyu, and used in following years as a venue for imperial receptions. It became the site of the first western-style stone building in Japan – a long demolished state guest house where former American president Ulysses S. Grant stayed in 1879. Handed to the city in 1945, Hama Rikyu Garden was opened to the public in 1946.

The garden's main feature, a seawater tidal pond, and its surrounds cover about 25 hectares (62 acres). Grass areas around the pond are punctuated with artificial hills, stands of trees and special features such as duck-hunting ponds and woods, a flower garden and a picnic area. Bridges link shores to an island-based pavilion named Ochaya, a focal point to many views across the pond.

E11 *Hama Rikyu is about 15 minutes' walk from Shimbashi station. Water buses connect with Asakusa from a wharf in the north-east corner.*

Kiyosumi Garden

Tokyo • Meiji Period

· ·

Huge stepping stones provide a wonderful spot for people to bring children to watch fish and stripey turtles.

Iwasaki Yataro built Kiyosumi Garden between 1878 and 1885 on the site of a run-down estate just east of the Sumida River. He constructed a lake, drew water from the Sumida River and transported rocks from sources all over Japan in Mitsubishi boats. These often massive rocks from as far away as Sendai, Sado, Shikoku and Kyushu give Kiyosumi Garden an exceptional character among Tokyo's relatively stoneless gardens.

Views from around the lake take in a *tsurujima* and other wooded islands, an azalea-clad hill called Fujimiyama or Tsutsujiyama (Azalea Hill), and Ryotei, a *sukiya*-style pavilion built over the water to honour the visit of Field Marshal Kitchener from England in 1907. Most striking is Isowatari, a seashore crossing made with stepping stones of monumental proportions, linking one island to the mainland. While Kiyosumi Garden was badly damaged during the Great Kanto Earthquake of 1923, it did provide life-saving protection for those who fled there. Noting its importance as a disaster refuge, the Iwasaki family donated the least damaged part, over 4 hectares (10 acres), to the city in 1924. The garden was restored and opened to the public in 1932.

E12 *Kiyosumi Garden is about 10 minutes' walk from Morishita station on the Toei Shinjuku subway line, or 20 minutes from Monzen-Nakacho on the Tozai line. Entrance is on the north side.*

Nezu Institute of Fine Arts

Tokyo • Showa Period

. . . .

The Nezu Institute of Fine Arts opened in 1941, the year after the death of founder Nezu Kaichiro, a successful business man (founder of the Tobu railway company) and prodigious art collector. It houses over 7000 works including paintings, calligraphy, sculptures, ceramics, lacquer works, textiles, metal works, Chinese bronzes from the Shang and Zhou dynasties and other oriental artworks. Present buildings date from 1954 and 1991, when a gallery was added to commemorate the Institute's fiftieth anniversary.

The Nezu Institute's friendly garden is built on a hillside falling to a long narrow pond. Leafy interlocking paths and steps link scenic spots, tea houses, shelters and other structures, lanterns and pagodas. While it seems a hybrid of western circulation patterns and eastern artefacts, it presents an enchanting hidden world, combining with the gallery as one of Tokyo's most attractive and rewarding destinations.

E13 *Closed Mondays. Nearest subway station is Omotesando on the Chiyoda Line*

Meiji Shrine Iris Garden

Tokyo • Meiji Period

. . . .

Emperor Meiji is said to have planned the iris garden built in the inner precincts of the Meiji Shrine in 1894 for the pleasure of the Empress. The garden contains 1500 plants of 150 species, growing in a serpentine, river-like bed of stepped shallow terraces hemmed in both sides by tall trees. Crossed in two places by low bridges, the iris river empties into a pond where water lilies grow. Azaleas and wisteria complement the garden's floral vocabulary. A path, following the line of terraces along one side between the bridges, provides the main flower-viewing space. The atmosphere is self-contained, like a narrow tended valley in a wood; there is no sense of the city here. The irises are probably best in the second half of June, when viewers crush into the meandering path to outnumber the plants.

E14 *About 10 minutes' walk from Harajuku station on the Yamanote Line. Walk up Meiji Jingu's great drive: the garden's entrance is on the left, after the second torii.*

Imperial Palace East Garden

Tokyo • Edo Period

. . . .

Tokugawa Ieyasu chose the site of an earlier castle, erected by Ota Dokan in 1457, for his Edo stronghold in 1590 and set about constructing, within a cocoon of concentric moats and over 1.8 square kilometres (450 acres) of elevated land, the walls and fortresses of a great castle. At its heart was Honmaru (Principal Fortress), which included the donjon, halls of state, the shogun's residence and other apartments. At the foot of Honmaru was Ninomaru (Second Fortress) with gardens, tea houses and a retirement palace, while to the south-west was Nishinomaru (West Fortress) and to the north was Kitanomaru. Repeated destruction by fires has left few remains today: only three of twenty-one watchtowers, some gates and massive stone walls.

The shogunate fell in 1867, the emperor was restored to power and the Imperial Palace was established in the grounds of Nishinomaru. The imperial private garden, the Fukiage garden, is reported to be the finest in Japan but seen only by select dignitaries. Some of Kitanomaru was sliced off for urban development, and land formerly occupied by Honmaru and Ninomaru was converted to a public park in 1968 to commemorate completion of the new Imperial Palace. Honmaru is landscaped with lawn areas, broad walks, masses of trees and hedges. A pond in the north-east corner of Ninomaru was once part of a garden attributed to Kobori Enshu, and described in its prime as more beautiful than Katsura.

E15 Enter through Otemon, the gate at the end of Eitai-dori. Enter by 15.00. Admission free. Enter Ninomaru by turning right by the guardhouses at the bend in the drive. Honmaru is further on, after the drive turns left, past another guard house and then through a gate opening on the right.

Visitors flock to photograph irises in full bloom in early June.

Horikiri Shobuen

Tokyo • Edo Period

· ·

Horikiri Shobuen. An iris oasis in hot Tokyo suburbia.

*A*farmer named Kodaka Izaemon is said to have first cultivated irises in swampy riverside land at Horikiri village in the 1660s. A descendant introduced new hybrid varieties of *hanashobu* early in the nineteenth century and opened the Kodaka Garden publicly. Cheerful parties of flower viewers would travel here from Edo, among them Hiroshige, who included the woodblock *Horikiri no hanashobu* in his *One Hundred Views of Famous Places in Edo* series.

Europeans and Americans also discovered the *hanashobu*. An export boom followed and the number of local gardens producing bulbs grew to five by the turn of the century. Demand fell away in the 1920s after the establishment of cultivation in the west; by 1942 only two gardens remained at Horikiri, and both were turned over to food production during the war. Horikiri Shobuen, as the old Kodaka Garden is now called, was re-opened in 1960.

E16 *About 8000 square metres (2 acres) in area, Horikiri Shobuen grows some six thousand irises of two hundred species along with other plants and trees. The best time to visit is mid-June. Admission free. The garden is 10 minutes' walk south from Horikiri Shobuen station on the Keisei Line.*

Kenchoji

Kamakura • Kanagawa Prefecture • Kamakura Period

· ·

Rankei Doryu, the Chinese priest who introduced 'pure' Sung-style Zen Buddhism to Japan, founded Kenchoji in 1253 with the patronage of regent Hojo Tokiyori. The first buildings were Chinese in style, but these and others were mostly destroyed by fires in the fourteenth and fifteenth centuries. Although rebuilt in the Edo period, many halls were destroyed in the Kanto earthquake of 1923. The Hojo, formerly the chief priest's residence but now the main hall, was moved here from its original location in Kyoto.

The garden behind the Hojo, attributed to Muso Soseki by the temple, was extensively modified during the Edo reconstruction. A pond, named Shinji-ike or Mind Character Pond for its shape, has water entering through a bamboo spout set in thick foliage on the extreme right. The pond is split in half by an earth bridge. The right-hand side contains a turtle island; the left has a peninsula, an island and a rock islet. A strong *horaisan* on the far bank provides a focal point.

Kenchoji's moss-encrusted lantern.

E17 *Expecting grassy banks, we were disappointed in mid-November to see bare earth. Greenest in summer, the garden would probably peak with spring azaleas. From Kita-Kamakura station, head back towards Kamakura along the main road; the side road to Kenchoji is clearly marked. About 20 minutes' walk. Kamakura is a popular recreation spot for Tokyoites, attracting large weekend and holiday crowds.*

Shonandai Cultural Centre

Shonandai • Kanagawa Prefecture • Heisei Period

. . . .

This fantasy garden delights child patrons.

Designed by Hasegawa Itsuko, the Shonandai Cultural Centre is simultaneously a garden and a joyous piece of contemporary architecture. Hasegawa sees architecture as 'another nature', massing her complex of spheres, undulating clusters of pyramid roofs, plaza and pool into an urban restatement of a mountain and valley landscape.

A planetarium in a suspended globe and a dome-covered auditorium combine with other functions over five levels. The Centre's public plaza, achieved by locating two floors underground, is also a hardy synthetic garden featuring a winding stream.

Plaza surfaces including those of the stream and its stepping stones are made of square grey tiles, the trees and bridges of polished silver metal. Details here invite playful response and demonstrate Hasegawa's delicate touch. The stream threads through the plaza to a deep, tiled pond with seaside imagery. Gardens planted with small trees and bushes are arranged on higher levels in a 'go-round' style; bushes in one area are clipped to echo pyramids found in nearby roof forms.

E18 *Shonandai is on the Odakyu/Enoshima Line, several stops from Fujisawa where this line interchanges with the JR Tokaido line. The centre can be seen from the station, only a few minutes walk away.*

Tokoji

Kofu • Yamanashi Prefecture • Kamakura Period

· ·

Rankei Doryu converted a Shingon Sect temple named Kokoku-in to a Zen temple in 1268, renaming it Kokoku Zenji. The temple was rebuilt as Tokoji in the Muromachi period. Only the Buddha hall survived subsequent vicissitudes to be declared an Important Cultural Property; other structures are post-war reconstructions. The garden is believed to have been built about 1270 and modified in the Edo period.

A pond, formed after the ideogram for dragon, lies between the temple and a hillside rugged with rock arrangements implying some vast mountainous territory, in the manner of Chinese ink paintings. The main design creates a long watercourse, commencing under the shade of background trees as a *karedaki* with a *rigyoseki* at its foot. It descends as dry rapids to a small rock-lined pool raised above the pond, then as a three-tiered cascade into the pond itself. Left of the

Tokoji's boat rock sails away in the centre, its side marked in stylised waves. A *karedaki* vanishes back in the shade.

karedaki a single mountain-shaped rock and subsidiary groups suggest a Shumisen group. The boat rock lying in the pond to the right of these rock groups restores balance to the overall design, and adds detailed foreground interest.

E19 *Several attractive modern gardens complement the approach to Tokoji's historic garden, as well as one in a small courtyard. The temple is in a grape-growing area about 1.5 kilometres (1 mile) from Kanente, the first local station east of Kofu. Turn right on the north side of the station, walk about 200 metres/yards then turn north towards the freeway and the TDK building. Turn right just before the road enters a tunnel and the temple is at the end of the road. (See map E19)*

Erinji

Enzan • Yamanashi Prefecture • Kamakura Period

. . . .

In this summer-pretty garden, a carefully trained pine stretches across the centre island, amidst a riot of flowers.

uso Soseki founded Erinji in 1330 when he converted a private mountain retreat and garden into a Zen temple. The present garden, while attributed to him, is thought to combine many alterations, including those made in the Edo period when the temple was rebuilt after being torched by forces of Oda Nobunaga in 1582.

Viewed from the main hall, Erinji's spacious hill and pond layout builds to a climax in the north-west corner where five rocks, assembled into an apparently single mountain-shaped rock, crown an artificial mountain. Other rocks tumble down the mountainside and a waterfall spills delicately just right of an arched stone bridge, but the mountain vastness implied in these constructions is compromised by an overscaled (and probably later) pagoda-style lantern on the summit. The pond's *nakajima* (central island) carries a striking horizontally trained pine tree; there is a similar tree on a bank nearby. The garden extends east with a narrow stream cutting between rocks and clipped azaleas, passing along the way under a chunky stone bridge. Light-filtering trees wrap around the garden, isolating it from the outside world.

E20 *Enzan is seven stops east of Kofu on JR Chuo Main Line. Take a bus from the station — about 10 minutes.*

Ryutanji

Kiga • Shizuoka Prefecture • Edo Period

. . . .

Temple information attributes the garden to Kobori Enshu (1579–1647) but some authorities think it was probably built in about 1676 when the main hall was reconstructed after a fire. Ryutanji's narrow pond resembles the heart ideogram and lies north of the hall. Mounding behind the pond is modelled into three mountain ranges covered in grass and rounded azalea bushes, and articulated with valleys carrying robust dry-waterfall rock formations. A *kamedejima* (turtle peninsula) lies at the foot of the middle range, there is a *tsurudejima* (crane peninsula) at the bottom of the western range, and

Two *karedaki* cascade among azaleas in valleys down each side of the central hill triad.

a rock *horai* island lies between them. A *sanzon* stone group just below the middle range summit resolves the overall design and provides the garden's focal point. Other noteworthy rocks include 'guardian stones' at each end of the pond, and a meditation stone on the southern bank.

E21 *Kiga is around 15 minutes from Mikkabi on the Tenryu-Hamana-ko line. (See Makayaji.) Buses passing the temple leave from the left side of the street leading away from Kiga-ekimae; service is infrequent. A taxi ride takes about 10 minutes. The bus stop below the main entrance to the temple complex posts a return timetable.*

Makayaji

Mikkabi • Shizuoka Prefecture • Heian or Kamakura Period

• •

Makayaji's sharply articulated yet sensuous garden, re-discovered in 1968, is a restoration of a late Heian- or early Kamakura-period garden, near the present-day temple buildings.

The garden's calm repose stems from the balance achieved between soft mountain curves and dense, angular, ruggedly textured rocks. In front of massed trees, the undulating forms of three grass-covered artificial mountains curve smoothly around a pond fed by a stream entering in the north-east. Crisp rock triads and other formations liberally stud these grassy slopes and the central crane island.

These rocks are particularly expressive in the crane grouping, where each aspect of the dominant triad presents a dynamically balanced synthesis. The crane's head is powerfully depicted by a long rock emerging horizontally from the pond's surface. A turtle peninsula thrusts from the south-west shore, tilting its head towards the island as if chasing the crane.

E22 *From Toyohashi on the* shinkansen *route take the JR Tokaido line train to Shinjohara. Transfer to the private Tenryu-Hamana-ko line; Mikkabi is about 20 minutes away through attractive rural scenery. From the station, the walk is about 30 minutes through the town to the temple.*

On the left, a foreground *kamedejima* looks towards the central crane island.

Eihoji

Tajimi • Gifu Prefecture • Kamakura Period

The bridge Musaikyo

E23 *Tajimi is on the JR Chuo Main Line, ex Nagoya. Eihoji is not far from a bus route starting at the station, but buses are infrequent and a taxi takes only about 10 minutes. (See map E23)*

Eihoji dates from 1312 when a monk called Gen'o Hongen, together with Muso Soseki and other monks, formed a hermitage on the site. The garden is sometimes attributed to Soseki, but might post-date his time there.

An arched bridge known as Musaikyo leads to the Kannon Hall (a National Treasure). Nearby leafy surrounds are interrupted by a fissured rock face, the setting for a waterfall and a group of small deity figures which rise theatrically from crevices and ledges. Eihoji's garden shows similarities to paradise gardens, suggesting a transitional development between the Heian-period style and the emergence of characteristic Zen Buddhist gardens.

Urakuen

Inuyama • Aichi Prefecture • Showa Period

Oda Uraku (1547–1621), brother of warlord Oda Nobunaga, retired late in life to Kenninji in Kyoto where he built a *shoin* and tea house in the sub-temple of Shoden-in. The tea house, named Jo-an, has been reconstructed at Urakuen, where it is the main attraction and a National Treasure. Tea gardens, delicately crafted and intimate, are set within an outer zone linking different themes and moods – one a garden of many varieties of tea, another a bamboo grove.

E24 *Urakuen is located in the Meitetsu Inuyama Hotel grounds, about 4 minutes' walk east of Inuyama castle.*

Kenrokuen

Kanazawa • Ishikawa Prefecture • Edo Period

. . . .

The Maeda clan, rulers of the Kaga district in the Edo Period, commenced building Kenrokuen in the early seventeenth century and completed it nearly two hundred years later. Kenrokuen became a public park in 1871 and is generally regarded as one of the finest surviving daimyo gardens. 'Kenrokuen' means Garden Displaying Six Qualities, namely spaciousness, seclusion, human artistry, maturity, plentiful water and fine vistas.

The garden is built on two levels over about 10.5 hectares (26 acres) separated by a road from the remaining structures of Kanazawa Castle, to which it was once the outer garden. The upper plateau contains a broad pond known as Kasumi-ga-ike, or Misty Lake, with a *horai* island. On the pond's edge the famous two-legged Kotoji lantern stands with one leg on land, one in the water. ('Kotoji' refers to the bridge supporting the strings of a *koto*.) Streams of many moods, sometimes broad and open, sometimes intimate, overhung with trees and planted out with irises, wind throughout the garden. One stream feeds the dramatic Midori-taki, or Green Waterfall, that spills into the lower Hisago-ike, or Gourd Lake. Ponds and streams are supplied with water from an elevated river some 10 kilometres (6.2 miles) away through a system of underground channels.

Kenrokuen offers a winter specialty brought about by the region's heavy snowfalls. The pine-trees near Kasumi-ga-ike are braced by straw ropes suspended from central poles like giant umbrella stays from November on.

E25 *Buses 10, 12, and 16 leaving from Kanazawa station pass Kenrokuen. Maps of Kanazawa are available in the information office at the back of JR ticket sales. Informative English language pamphlets are handed out to ticket purchasers. Expect crowds if you are not there early or late in the day, or off season.*

Watery reflections of cherry blossom filter among delicate green young iris plants in a stream.

Gyokusenen

Kanazawa • Ishikawa Prefecture • Edo Period

· ·

Wakita Naokata, founder of Gyokusenen, was captured as a child in the Korean invasion and taken into service with the Maeda family. He eventually became chamberlain to the second lord, Toshinaga, and married into the Wakita family, whose name he was granted. The garden honours Gyokusen-in, Toshinaga's wife. It is entered at the lower of two levels. Stepping stones ascend a leafy hillside to the Saisetsutei Roji, featuring a pond and a very old pine tree wrapped with climbing trumpet flowers. A replica of the Kanuntei tea room at the Ura-Senke School of Tea in Kyoto overlooks the lower pond.

E26 *Gyokusenen lies east of Kenrokuen, on a street running east from Hyakumangoku-dori. Closed in winter.*

Nomura Residence

Kanazawa • Ishikawa Prefecture • Edo Period (Showa reconstruction)

· ·

A rivulet busy with colorful carp.

The Nagamachi neighbourhood in Kanazawa retains some of its former samurai-quarter atmosphere; this reconstructed house is open to the public as an illustration of traditional culture. Beginning c 1600, Nomura ownership of the property continued for ten generations until the Meiji Restoration dismantled the samurai profession. A new owner transported a reception room from an old house in southern Ishikawa Prefecture, and reconstructed it overlooking an attractive garden.

A winding stream skirts the narrow verandah. Integration of house and garden is established by a deep roof overhang that extends over the stream, and emphasised at floor level where flat-topped smooth rocks provide textural connections with the verandah's polished boards.

E27 *Lying near the Saigawa river. See maps available from the information office at JR Kanazawa station.*

Heisenji

Katsuyama • Fukui Prefecture • Muromachi Period

. . . .

According to legend, a Buddhist priest named Taicho decided to live a life of prayer and meditation at the foot of Hakusan in 717. In a vision Kannon, the Goddess of Mercy, arising from a forest spring, ordered him to worship the mountain as dwelling of the gods. He responded by building a shrine, which also functioned as the Heisenji Buddhist temple. Heisenji grew to a great complex with thirty-six temples, forty-eight shrines and a population of more than six thousand monks during the Muromachi period. Supported by its army of eight hundred soldier monks, Heisenji engaged in power struggles that eventually led to its total destruction in 1574 by another Buddhist sect. Rebuilt on a smaller scale, Heisenji never again exercised secular power.

So thick, lush and all-pervasive is the moss carpet at Heisenji that the temple has earned the nickname 'Moss Palace'. The surrounding mossy expanse under towering cedar trees gives Heisenji its great charm, but a garden of detailed interest is the relatively small Old Genjo in Garden (about 1000 square metres or 1200 square yards) which adjoins a residence lying west of the ascending pathway to the main hall. It was designed by a landscape gardener named Hosokawa Takakuni in the late Muromachi period. Little of his original elaborations remains; today the garden's beauty lies in dense swards of moss in some thirty-six species, occasionally interrupted by rocks or stepping stones. It has been declared a National Scenic Spot by the Japanese Government.

E28 *From Fukui, Katsuyama is at the end of the Echizen Main Line of the Keifuku Dentetsu Railway. At the station, transfer to the Keifuku bus bound for Heisenji. Get off at Heisenji Jinja-mae after a 15-minute trip. If walking, cross the river, turn right through the town's shopping street, then left towards the hills until a major highway (route 157) and the castle can be seen. Take the road that runs past the castle's north side. Heisenji is a little further on, to the right, just after a road junction. (See map E28)*

Sun-dappled moss lies as a carpet between tall trees.

Asakura Family Residential Ruins

Ichijodani (near Fukui) • Fukui Prefecture • Muromachi Period

Enduring relics of a temple garden on the fringe of thick forest.

The Asakura clan established a castle town in a broad, defensible valley along the Ichijodani river in the years between 1471 and 1573 (when the clan was overwhelmed by Oda Nobunaga). The site is now a Special National Historic Landmark. Gravel compounds and foundation stones mark out dwellings once strung along the valley floor, and five gardens in or near the eastern slopes have been partially restored.

The ruins of the main villa lie in a hedged compound now marked by a 'Chinese-style' gate supposedly offered by Toyotomi Hideyoshi as a memorial to Yoshikage, the last Asakura lord. Of its two gardens, one has a compact pond and waterfall design, backing against a steep hillside. The other, a stone-edged rectangle in a nearby courtyard, is 'the oldest flower garden in Japan', or so a bystander translated his guide's remarks.

The other gardens lie on higher land along the side of the valley. A rock-strewn grassy depression, once a pond garden, lies just above the villa site and a mossy, sculptural ruin nestles against dense forest further north along a narrow trail. The largest garden, on a small plateau south of the main villa, is the most completely restored. It is a pond and waterfall composition dominated by a splendid towering rock, overhung by golden leaves in autumn. This garden was built after 1568 at the house of Yoshikage's mistress Shosho no Tsubone.

E29 *The site – beautiful in a moody, slightly melancholy way on an autumn day when ginkgoes flared against dark hillsides, mists shrouded mountain tops and rain squalls swept up the valley – would be memorable in any season. It can be reached by occasional JR trains from Fukui to Ichijodani station and then walking, but more frequent buses return from the car-park and rest room complex.*

Golden autumn at Shosho no Tsubone's ancient garden.

Shibata Residence

Tsuruga • Fukui Prefecture • Edo Period

. . . .

The residence built by Shibata Mitsuari and his son Kiyonobu in stages from 1662 overlooks a pond across a steeply sloping pebble shore. An island within the pond is connected to banks by earth-covered log bridges. Clipped bushes, mainly azaleas, spread across background slopes and the garden is enclosed by hedges and trees, which part in one place to frame a view of distant mountains.

A number of the garden's fine rocks have crisply delineated vertical and horizontal surfaces echoed in the cubic forms of bushes intermingling with more usual rounded ones. The profusion of azaleas suggests that the scene would be most attractive in the ambience of late spring to early summer, with fresh greens and pinks reflected in a clear pond. In a rather casual garden extension around the far side of the house, a small stream meanders between trees and stands of bamboo.

E30 *Take the bus from 2 bus stop in front of Tsuruga station. Get off at Ichinono, after about 12 minutes. The house is just ahead. (See map E30)*

Saifukuji

Tsuruga • Fukui Prefecture • Edo Period

. . . .

Shogun Ashikaga Yoshimitsu assisted in the establishment of Saifukuji in 1368 at the end of a small valley on the outskirts of present-day Tsuruga. Designated a Place of Scenic Beauty, the existing garden was built in the middle Edo period. Some of the buildings now standing show signs of dilapidation; the picturesque garden seems to have fallen from an earlier glorious state, and industrial Japan is only two or three rice fields away. Yet in these reduced circumstances the temple wears a certain weathered nobility, as if time has added character lines to an earlier perfection.

64

The garden has two levels at the foot of a wild ravine behind a relatively new study hall. The higher area is a small, grassy plateau in front of a grotto. Water trickles from the grotto's roof to its floor, runs around the plateau as a small stream, then falls into a pond that rambles across the main lower level to lap under an elevated corridor. The pond, with an overgrown dry waterfall to its left, has a central cluster of three islands and several bridges, some in seeming disrepair. Clipped bushes, rocks and lanterns decorate slopes and banks. Ravine and garden are united in an exhilarating, expansive design through the relationship of garden rocks to vistas of natural outcrops, accompanied by an interplay between manicured plants and untrammelled nature.

Saifukuji's garden recedes into a wooded hillside.

E31 *Take the bus to Matsubacho from stop 1 in front of Tsuruga station. After passing through the main business district and crossing a river, the bus passes a thick belt of pines on the right; get off just before the main road turns right. Follow a narrow road ahead that dog-legs through suburban houses and turn right at the first major intersection. Cross a small river and you will see the roofs of Saifukuji just beyond a large factory.* (See map E30)

Daitsuji

Nagahama • Shiga Prefecture • Edo Period

D aitsuji's two gardens were constructed between 1751 and 1780 during the tenure of the fifth priest, Shino Shonin. Old photographs displayed at the temple show that the dry garden known as Ganzanken once contained a pond. A bold *karedaki*, partly hidden by foliage, appears to the left. A crane island links to the right-hand shore line via a small stone bridge. On clear days a view of Mt Ibuki is framed by background and flanking trees of carefully controlled heights. The Rantei garden, a *karesansui* composition in a courtyard, features rocks disposed as precipitous mountain scenery in the Chinese ink-painting style. The scale of these rocks in a small space has a power reminiscent of Daisen-in. Daitsuji's gardens are worth visiting for the strength of their stone groups and compositional interest.

Daitsuji's fissured mountain rock is distinctly Chinese in feeling. Hazy sky conceals *shakkei* of Mt Ibuki.

E32 *The temple is about 10 minutes' walk from Nagahama station. Walk down the main street leading away from the station and turn left just before the road crosses a river (the temple is well signed at this point). Turn right, then left again and Daitsuji is at the end of an attractive shopping street lined with small-scale, traditionally styled buildings.*

Genkyuen

Hikone • Shiga Prefecture • Edo period

. . . .

Ii Nao-oki, fourth lord of the daimyo family, built a garden alongside a detached palace at the base of Hikone castle in 1677, about fifty-five years after the castle's completion. Now called Genkyuen, the 2-hectare (5-acre) garden displays in design details and bold rock groups a style canon reminiscent of the Momoyama period.

The garden lies beside wooded slopes rising to Hikone Castle, with the Tenshukaku (Main Castle Tower) prominent on the western skyline. A large pond contains four islands, two at the southern end linked by timber bridges in a bent-axis arrangement. The *horai* island in the northern part of the pond dramatically sites a tall rock at the water's edge before a large clipped evergreen tree that may represent the immortals' mountain dwelling. Pavilions on the west side, some overlapping the water, offer superb views across the pond.

An exceptionally dramatic *horai* island composition is the focal point looking from the shore below the castle.

Hikone Castle looms above Genkyuen and its pond.

E33 *Admission to the garden is included with the admission ticket to Hikone Castle, a short walk from Hikone Station.*

Ryotanji

Hikone • Shiga Prefecture • Edo Period

Ryotanji's *karesansui* garden.

The Ii family temple since 1055, Ryotanji was established on its present site in 1601 after Naomasa became first lord of Hikone. Buildings were completed in 1617, when Naotaka was second lord. The temple has two interesting gardens, one a *karesansui* garden, the other a pond garden making excellent use of a natural gully as borrowed scenery.

The dry Hojo South Garden is a rectangular space formed by temple structures on two sides, and elsewhere separated by low hedges from natural woodland. Three islands of moss and rocks lie in an ocean of raked sand, the central island symbolising Fudaraku Mountain, spiritual home of Kannon, Goddess of Mercy. The Shoin East Garden pond lies at the foot of a compact hillside thickly covered with rocks and clipped bushes that merge with the gully's natural foliage. An expressive rock turtle island in the pond directs its head towards a crane peninsula at the foot of a generally dry waterfall; a rock in the fall's lower levels suggests a *rigyoseki*.

E34 *Ryotanji is 20 minutes' walk from Hikone station; the Tourist Information Centre outside the station has maps.*

Daichiji

Minakuchi • Shiga Prefecture • Edo Period

• •

The present temple was established in 1667 on a site where one is said to have existed since the eighth century. The *karesansui* garden east of the *shoin* displays one of Japan's most striking examples of *o-karikomi*. Legend attributes its design to Kobori Enshu, who died in 1647; one of his students seems more likely.

The central focus is a sinuously coiled azalea hedge said to represent a treasure ship sailing the seas around a *horai* island. Azaleas in its centre are clipped to depict sails,

The great azalea hedge, allowed to outgrow its precise form; the azaleas are about to bloom.

others are treasure boxes. Hedges at different levels to the rear undulate in wave formations. A clipped bush close to the *shoin* represents a turtle island.

On the west another garden contains a pine tree over three hundred years old, its heavy, horizontally trained form is said to resemble a reclining dragon. In front of the tea room a deep, narrow garden leads to a white-walled storehouse. These gardens also feature *o-karikomi*.

E35 *Minakuchi is on the Omi-Tetsudo line ex Maibara – change trains at Yokaichi. The trip takes about 75 minutes. The walk to Daichiji takes about 30 minutes. (See map E35)*

Enman-in

Otsu • Shiga Prefecture • Edo Period

Yellow leaves drift over Enman-in's garden on a peaceful autumn afternoon.

*E*nman-in has a *shinden*-style main hall donated by Empress Meisho, moved from the Imperial Palace in 1641. Its garden was probably built about the same time.

A long pond with a narrow bank of gravel, grass and clipped bushes lies parallel to the main hall. Successive views through the shoji openings look across to a steep, thickly wooded hillside. Moving from left to right, there is firstly a crane island to the east, connected to the near and far banks by stone bridges, one surfaced with a delicate mossy patina. A turtle island lies near the pond's centre; on the opposite side, a rock symbolising Mt Horai forms a tripartite composition with two islands. There is a rather overgrown dry waterfall at the western end above the entry of a natural stream.

E36 *Enman-in is about 10 minutes' walk from Nishi-Otsu station, on JR Kosei Line from Kyoto. Walk south down the main road, take the second road on the right (not counting the road opposite the station), then the first left. Enman-in is off to the right, about mid-block.*

Koshoji

Kutsuki • Shiga Prefecture • Muromachi Period

Inter-twined, a tree and the great *tsurujima* wing rock.

Once belonging to Shurinji, a temple destroyed by fire and abandoned in the eighteenth century, this fascinating 'ruined' garden lies in front of present-day Koshoji, but it was in fact the garden for a sixteenth-century villa where shogun Ashikaga Yoshiharu stayed for some time after fleeing from an attack on Kyoto in 1528. It certainly seems detached from the temple and its concerns.

The remains are situated on a small plateau overlooking a cultivated and lightly built valley. Weathered rocks, many of strong individual character, define pond and islands. The pond meanders south from a small waterfall in the north-west corner, around a *kamejima* bearing a *horai* rock, under a stone bridge and around a *tsurujima* with a wonderfully powerful wing. Old gnarled trees grow here and there. The garden has the casual look of a naturally occurring brook – there is little of the usual artifice and visitors can walk around quite freely.

E37 *Take buses for Kutsuki from the west side of Adogawa station on JR Kosei Line, a pleasant trip up Lake Biwa from Kyoto. After the trip through a rural valley – another travel treat – get off at Kutsuki-gakko-mae (high school). Check return bus times at the bus stop (very infrequent after school hours). Walk straight ahead up the valley along a road through rice fields, through a small hamlet, and turn right at the Jizo statue (about 10 minutes' walk). You can enter the garden freely, but we thought it polite to visit the temple.*

Jizo-in

Seki • Mie Prefecture • Edo Period

· ·

Visitors coming to Jizo-in to see its famous Jizo *bodhisattva*, said to be the oldest in Japan, may also enjoy a small overgrown garden built behind the temple during the middle Edo period.

We visited Jizo-in on a dark, wet day near the end of spring when carmine azaleas gleamed among dripping jade and emerald leaves overhanging the low-lying pond beside the verandah. This heart-ideogram-shaped pond is crossed by a stone bridge while, looming beneath the greenery on its far side, half-concealed rocks sprawl down a high artificial mound. Lanterns peep out among azaleas, bush clover, maples and the plant profusion along the banks. Because of reconstruction, little of the garden was available for photography.

E38 *A post town on the Tokaido road in the Edo period, Seki has been declared a preservation district for its groups of historic buildings. Our unorthodox route from Tsu involved the wrong temple and a very wet walk, but Jizo-in is near Seki station on JR Kansai Main Line. Turn west along the road parallel to the railway on the north side, then take the road running north-west. Vegetarian lunch is served.*

Isuien

Nara • Nara Prefecture • Meiji Period

· ·

A textile merchant built the small west garden here in the 1670s, but more notable is the eastern addition, completed by a wealthy merchant in 1899, capturing the roof of Nandaimon, Todaiji's Great South Gate, and the hills of Nara in a spectacular exhibition of *shakkei*.

Built in front of a thatch-roofed pavilion called Sanshutei (Pavilion of Three Beauties), the intimate older garden contains a pond with crane and turtle islands. Around a tea arbour to the east, the scenery of the added garden extends in a rising vista. From near Hyoshintei (Pavilion of the Frozen Heart), a sweeping composition employs borrowed scenery

· ·

in an expansive four-layered conception that moves from the pond via a lavishly planted garden hillside and the tops of woods near Himuro Shrine to the distant profiles of Wakakusayama and Mt Kasuga, while framing the roof of Nandaimon. A row of stepping stones across the pond provides continuity with the first owner; they are said to be milling stones he used in preparing sizing for ramie cloth.

E39 *Isuien lies on the western edge of Nara Park. Walk down the main street towards the park from Kintetsu Nara station, turn left on the main road to Kyoto (route 369). Take the first right and Isuien is ahead to the left.*

Late spring serenity at Isuien.

To-in Teien

Nara • Nara Prefecture • Nara Period

Newly opened, a Nara-period garden restoration.

The reconstructed To-in Teien (East Palace Garden) brings to life a style that hitherto could be only visualised from descriptions in poems of the Nara period such as those found in the *Man'yoshu* and *Kaifuso* collections, which dwelt lyrically on the delights of pebbled shores, sunlight sparkling on dancing water and the tangled fine threads of green willows.

Uncovered in the south-east corner of the Heijo Palace site in 1967, the garden remains indicated a complicated pond formation, rock-strewn beaches and pavilions over a site of about 7000 square metres (1.7 acres). Excavations, surveys and construction followed for about thirty years. Finally the finished works, complete with pond, pavilions, bridges, young trees and enclosing walls, were opened to the public in 1998.

The pond seems to have been constructed in two stages during the Nara period. The earlier formation was defined by boulders as a long, narrow and reverse L-shape, more like a winding stream. Later this was changed to the broad and shallow pebble-lined pond that is seen today in the reconstruction.

E40 *Probably the easiest, and certainly the most interesting, way to get to To-in Teien is to take bus 12 or 13 from JR Nara station or Kintetsu Nara station (stop 13 on the north-bound road west of Kintetsu station) to Hokkeji-mae, then walk west, and south to the palace precinct. Closed Mondays and New Year holidays.*

Jiko-in

Yamato Koriyama • Nara Prefecture • Edo Period

. . . .

Katagiri Sadamasa (1615–1673), daimyo of Yamato Koizumi, also known as tea master Katagiri Sekishu, built Jiko-in in 1663 to honour his late father. Sadamasa had studied tea ceremony under priest Sohaku in Daitokuji, and his cultivated taste is apparent in the restrained elegance suffusing the *hojo* and its garden.

From a small entry gate, you approach the temple along a zig-zag progression of narrow leafy paths until, from the main gate, the thatch-roofed

The view from the drawing room.

hojo can be glimpsed at the end of a rustic stone path. A *karesansui* garden wraps around the south-east corner of the *hojo*, from where the Yamato plain and the eastern mountains of the Nara basin appear as borrowed scenery above a low hedge. Power-lines and buildings now disfigure this long-famous view but young pine trees rising above the hedge line suggest future screening. The most attractive part lies to the south, where large rounded azalea bushes and a few rocks evoke mountain scenery; their earth-hugging forms contrast beautifully with tall tree trunks growing from their midst. An extra enjoyment is freedom to leave the building and stroll about.

E41 *Jiko-in is about 20 minutes' walk in a north-westerly direction from Yamato Koizumi station on the Kansai Main Line from Nara. Head west from the station, turn right along the first road after crossing the river (not on the river bank), proceed to the next major east-west road, turn left and Jiko-in is a little further along on rising land on the right. The entrance fee includes tea, served in the drawing room overlooking the garden.*

Joruriji

Near Nara • Kyoto Prefecture • Heian Period

Joruriji's rustic simplicity suggests that to twelfth-century believers Amida's Western Paradise was not necessarily interpreted in terms flamboyant and vast, but could be visualised as homely, and tranquilly in tune with nature.

Joruriji is thought to have been founded some time in the Nara period. The present Amida hall, having been moved from another site, replaced an earlier hall in 1157. It enshrines nine

The old Amida hall drowses in late spring heat. Frogs croak, cicadas hum.

in-line images of Amida, and is sole survivor of more than twenty 'Nine–Amida halls' thought to have existed in the Heian period. The hall faces east over a large pond to a three-storey pagoda transferred from a temple in Kyoto in 1178, now housing the wooden statue of Yakushi Nyorai (Buddha of Healing), installed as principal deity in the original hall.

The Amida hall, the nine images of Amida and the pagoda are all National Treasures. Two remaining Guardian King statues are also National Treasures. Other statues and stone lanterns are Important Cultural Properties. The pond, excavated and restored to its original twelfth-century formation in 1976, is a charming foil for the Amida hall's graceful lines and those of its vertical counterpoint, the pagoda, in their rural setting.

E42 *Take bus 111 bound for Kamo-eki via Joruriji from stop 9 in front of the Nara JR station, or pick it up at stop 13 on the north-bound road west of Kintetsu Nara station. Buses run at two-hourly intervals (from 9.30 at JR station, but check times). The trip takes 25 minutes.*

4

VISITING THE
OLD CAPITAL

Kyoto: a short, sweet word plucked on a koto, summoning images from a gracious past – a lamp-lit room, the grassy scent of fresh tatami mats, birds skimming gilded paper, kimono-clad poets on silken cushions, moonlight and dark foliage beyond open shoji. Like that of Paris, Kyoto's very name summons a romantic aura: centuries of legend, history, passion and art distilled into two syllables.

The rich texture of history that accompanies Kyoto's former role as ancient capital gives it a unique role in Japan today. The city's loss of status with the Meiji confirmation of Edo as the capital Tokyo in 1869 in a curious way guaranteed its survival. Kyoto could have become a museum, a marvellous relic of sensitive traditional Japan, but it didn't quite turn out like that. A city must go on living or stagnate. Kyoto's central position and role as cultural guardian have ensured its continuing purpose in a country seething with alien economic imperatives, but the ancient structures to some extent have become graceful retreats among ticky-tacky as Kyoto inhabitants scrambled to catch up with post-war modernisation. And yet an extraordinary mix of old and new co-exists in a cultural vitality that continues the city's ancient legacy. Throughout all the changes wrought by economic pressures and tourism, Kyoto retains the allure of its history and the unsurpassed artistry of its architecture and its gardens.

A perfect marriage between a culture and its resources began with the capital's eighth-century move from Nara, where the court had become threatened by the very temples it had assisted to wealth. A wealthy landowner with court connections proffered a new site away from these annoyances: a tract of flat, fertile land conforming to geomantic requirements, with convenient provincial road links, and rivers for plentiful water. The beauty of Kyoto's surrounding hills, with their luxuriant forests and sparkling streams, must have influenced the emperor's decision, but probably fortuitous were the ready supplies of rocks and sand and the benefits of humid summers – for gardens, if not for humans. In this promising locale the 'Golden Age' of the Heian period evolved, the expression of a leisured aristocracy preoccupied with aesthetics and with the means to satisfy their tastes and the discrimination to achieve perfection.

At Shisendo, bamboo shelters the stone path: a quiet approach. Removing shoes, we step forward through the entrance rooms. Bright light explodes on white sand overhung by the great sasanqua. A lantern nestles between clipped green spheres of azalia; beyond, maples vermilion and yellow in the afternoon sun. Bittersweet brilliance of the dying season.

Kyoto never really filled its planned domain; the west languished while nobles and religious sects sought the picturesque foothills for villas and temples. The city that Toyotomi Hideyoshi began walling off in the late sixteenth century lay mostly east of the original central north–south axis (now Senbon-dori), while beyond the north boundary it had fanned out west of the Kamo River. Most of the long-lived gardens that now form the city's major attraction lie within this Kyoto and its nearby foothills. Here less frequented temples still retain a quieter ambience while in the valley historic relics are crowded among the shambles of a city that has escaped modern planning.

It is hard to write about the fable and frustration of Kyoto, a city where moments of heaven illuminate the downtown battleground. Much of the central area is crass, ugly or plain boring for all the usual modern city reasons, compounded here by a planning failure to integrate rational new development with preservation. Traffic nears gridlock in the main streets. Some forty thousand wooden townhouses were replaced with concrete offices or apartments in the ten years up to 1997 or simply torn down. Gouverneur Mosher in his 1964 *Contemplative Guide* bewailed the dwindling of the lost tram system, still extant on a 1972 visit. Since then the development industry has effectively carried out the destruction Kyoto was spared in the war. Theoretically left intact, the city was actually vulnerable to the piecemeal intervention that has brought some parts to a virtual standstill, unable to cope with its forty million tourists a year.

Kawaramachi, jam-packed at Sanjo, awash with bodies in a state of shopping frenzy, spilling out of the major arcades, teen meccas for gifts: slogan-screaming T-shirts, UFO stations, ukiyo-e of grimacing actors, Hello Kitty hairclips, imitation indigo ladieswear, yapping electronic pets . . . Only Shijo with its bulbous cream awnings is more crowded with shoppers at department stores from Daimaru to the Big Off.

In Central Kyoto the shopping arcades, roofed former streets, relieve the pedestrian pressures of so many visitors. Away from the main avenues the small-scale idiom of the old streetscape still partially survives, harbouring a chaotic mix of old and new. For all this hubbub the old magic described by Mosher re-asserts itself in many by-ways. Moments away from Kawaramachi the modern entertainment area merges into that of Pontocho, a sliver of a lane with traditional bars and restaurants secreted behind high walls and timber screens. In summer patrons carouse on balconies hung above the river and pairs of lovers line the embankment below at two-metre intervals. South of the downtown bustle the Takase River is a leafy link for a community that looks both ageless and relatively intact. East of the Kamo River, paths along garden-walled canals offer tranquil pedestrian refuge from busy roads. The eastern foothills are patterned with alleys leading from one temple to another, full of incident. Lanes of traditional small shops branch off in various directions and the slope up to Kiyomizu is lined with stalls selling fine crafts, sweet cakes and souvenirs. Around Gion the *geisha* quarter is full of tiny streets; even at busy Gion intersection it is only a step across into Maruyama Park, where rows of lanterns glow at night in the Yasaka Shrine.

Nijo Castle post-breakfast: just after 8 am and hot. Gorgeous gilt gleaming on the dark timber entrance gable, but kerb-to-kerb buses throng the forecourt. Elderly farmer groups from the provinces anxiously pursue their leaders while teenage multitudes scuff around in the dusty gravel, queuing for compulsory culture. Pavement impassable. Try again later. The same. Inside, behind closed shoji, feet thunder past treasures invisible through the mob, trampling the much-vaunted nightingale floors, whose delicately twittering boards warned the shogun of creeping intruders . . .

Vast hordes at Kinkakuji, 'keep moving' signs at Ginkakuji and shuffling feet and camera clicks at Ryoanji can destroy any meditative calm. Yet a visit to Kyoto should include these three iconic masterpieces as well as some quieter places like Entsuji, Rengeji, Toji-in, Taizo-in, Konchi-in, Chishaku-in, Koto-in, Tofukuji Hojo or Sesshu-in – beautiful gardens where crowds are rare. Daisen-in, Shisendo and Nanzenji Hojo seem to attract larger but not oppressive numbers. Just as old Kyoto can be sensed in suburbs and side streets, the essential, exquisite calm of a Japanese garden can still be experienced in quiet gardens away from tourist circuits and commercialised reverence. However it is sometimes better to accept crowding as a celebration of the human spectacle rather than a threat. You can become accustomed to it, we realised one day while negotiating the prime spot for a famous view with several others, practically touching, but secure in our reduced personal space.

The quintessential stone garden: Ryoanji suddenly empties, a rare moment of virtual solitude – lunchtime, when tours eat. Back-lit, the perfect plane of gravel is freshly raked, not a leaf in sight. Immaculate, overpowering perfection. The stones posing their eternal question.

Peak season is a major event in garden viewing – times like autumn almost anywhere, or cherry blossom time at Sambo-in, Tenryuji, or the Heian Shrine. These places are delightful at other times, but if you only seek quietness, you may just miss the reason for their fame. The extraordinary brilliance of maples at their peak, crimson and pale gold against blue sky, can bring tears. It is no wonder that ethereal clouds of cherry blossom induce beneath them diverse celebrations, from elegant poetry parties to modern office frolics.

8.30 am in sunny November: the bus queue for the country town of Ohara overflows its rank, tangling with commuters already harassed by the hoardings of Kyoto station, unfinished for years. The annual autumn leaf ritual is on. On the bus immaculate matrons sway tolerantly around us in a sardine density repeated later in Sanzen-in's narrow temple spaces, where the shuffling cavalcade pauses only for quick snaps. Stepping down into the garden, you have to be quick with shoes in case the next person falls into yours.

Three of Kyoto's finest gardens are those of the imperial estates, administered by the Imperial Household Agency. You are privileged to see these places at all, but the restrictions are sometimes too intrusive. At Katsura you rush past incomparable scenery, allowed to pause only at roomier spots with no famous view, stragglers prodded. The larger, park-like spaces of Shugakuin and Sento Gosho are much more relaxed, being less intensive and perhaps less in demand. Both are impressive and rewarding, the former for its exquisitely laid out grounds and backdrop of infinitely receding valleys, and the latter city garden for its perfectly orchestrated and maintained stroll sequences and immaculate pebble beach.

Back to town: late afternoon, stuffy bus. Camera bags clutched at chests, balanced above seated heads, we jolt down Higashioji-dori hip to hip at the back of a 206 bus. The ticket machine's up front, next stop we get off, there's no change – a moment for helpless panic or the application of brute force. Too polite to push forwards we contemplate being over-carried. With regardless determination, a tiny grandma furiously crashes through at waist level.

The keen photographer will encounter problems, as some wonderful gardens cannot be photographed. Unable to present them visually, we have omitted them from the individual descriptions but want to draw attention to them here. Sambo-in, for instance, at Daigoji, popular at cherry blossom time, has a lavish garden reconstructed by Toyotomi Hideyoshi. Elaborate banks and islands enhance a pond fed by a three-step waterfall, and spanned by stone, timber and earth-covered bridges. Many fine trees, bushes and about seven hundred rocks, one reputed to be worth five thousand bushels of rice, make an opulent display of Momoyama bravura. Others in this category are Entsuji, and Shuon-an. The latter has a dramatic *karesansui* composition north of the *hojo* in the ink-painting style, climaxing in one corner in a massive mountainous rock heading a two-tier waterfall, surrounded by more rock mountains and valleys. The narrow garden on the east side has rocks in a 7–5–3 arrangement among low shrubs and trees, while the south garden is a simple plane of gravel backed by a bank of low clipped bushes and cycads, topped by a long, trimmed hedge.

Nishi Honganji is not quite in this group, you can photograph it, but the tour concentration is more on the brilliant Momoyama architecture particularly the Taimenjo (Audience Hall) with its exquisite decorated ceiling. This flanks the Kokei-no-Niwa or Tiger-glen Garden, believed, like the hall, to have been relocated from Hideyoshi's palace at Fushimi. In this further composition of Momoyama pictorial bravado, massive rocks define a distant mountain cascade, from which a stream flows around crane and turtle islands, linked by graceful monolithic stone bridges. We snatched a brief glimpse of the garden, its cycads straw-encased for winter, tilted among bold expressive rocks.

Entsuji: enthralled we sit gazing over the subtle variations of velvety moss, the coarser weaves of bushes and hedges, the rugged fabric of the treetops. Lost in distance shimmers the spun-silk blue-grey of distant Mt Hiei. A sumptuous array of textures, an experience of ineffable peace.

Moving around Kyoto is easy thanks to its efficient public transport system but some routes can be extremely crowded. Subway improvements with the recent Tozai line ease access to the eastern foothills, reducing crowded bus rides, like those involving Shijo, Kawaramachi and Higashioji. On the west side Horikawa can also offer a long slow ride.

During our garden travels the Kyoto station was disrupted for years by the building of the monumental new station edifice, whose lack of empathy for Kyoto's glorious past is breathtaking. Its extravagant self-aggrandisement can however in some sense be understood as providing a sophisticated new vision for Kyoto's inhabitants – or at least its city fathers, living as they do in a culturally pre-eminent city whose modern facilities are barely provincial. Meanwhile, relatively unchanged, the essential practicalities of ordinary shopping, eating and subway facilities, continue as before, beneath the new glamour stores and nightspots.

Young Kyoto haunts the new mini-city mega-structure atop the station, sipping drinks in its cavernous evening darkness, and riding the escalators to the top of the Daikaidan, ingenious store exit but grand stair to nowhere much other than consumer reveries and filet mignon with a view.

Kiyomizu at sunset: the western glow fades over the blue misting city, sparked with street lights. In the darkness of the temple depths, the old pendant iron lights, patterned black against opal, come on. Wandering in from the great wooden platform, we are dwarfed by giant beams lost above in ancient shadows. Only a few couples, motionless silhouettes against a champagne evening sky, linger in the last light.

Sambo-in and Entsuji are further described in Chapter 2. **K21** *For Sambo-in, take Tozai line to Diago station; walk north , then east.* **K24** *For Shuon-an, take the JR Gakkentoshi Line to Tanabe, or the Kintetsu Kyoto Line to Shintanabe. Buses leave both stations for Ikkyuji-michi bus stop. The temple is half a kilometre (500 yards) west of the stop.* **K36** *Nishi Honganji is a short walk from Kyoto station. Access is by guided tour; make bookings at the temple office.* **K38** *Entsuji is best seen on a clear day. Take bus 28 from the bus terminal at Kitaoji station to Entsuji-michi. Take the road running west to the temple.*

GARDENS IN KYOTO

GARDENS AT OHARA

K1 and K2

. . . .

The village of Ohara, located among beautiful hills and valleys north of Kyoto, is the setting for two historic temples with enticing gardens.

Each is within comfortable walking distance from the Ohara terminal for buses 17 and 18 from Kyoto station, and 16 from Sanjo-Keihan bus terminal. The bus trip from Kyoto takes about one hour.

Sanzen-in in autumn

Sanzen-in

Edo Period

· ·

Eshin (942–1017), the Tendai priest who advocated Nembutsu and made it popular with the aristocrats, built an Amida hall called Ojo-gokuraku-in, the Temple of Rebirth in Paradise, between two streams on the slopes of Gyosan (Fish Mountain) in 985. His Amida hall, rebuilt in 1143, now stands on the south side of a lovely garden.

Ojo-gokuraku-in in deepest winter.

The usual circulation route through Sanzen-in leads first around the verandahs of the Kyakuden (Reception Chamber), built 1587. The Shuhekien (Garden that Gathers Green – a rather fussy slope of hedges and clipped bushes rising above a small pond) bends around the south and east sides. Stairs and corridors lead to the Shinden, a 1926 reconstruction of the sixteenth-century original, where the south verandah overlooks the main garden known as Yuseien, or the Garden of Pure Presence. A sea of moss, punctuated by cryptomeria trunks, stretches ahead to Ojo-gokuraku-in. To the left is a small pond edged by low clipped bushes. This calm, tree-enclosed space is a perfect foil for the simple, weathered architecture of its focal point, and its beauty in the full blaze of autumn, or under snow, can be breathtaking.

K1 *Take a side road running east just north of Ohara bus terminal. Keep right at the next fork. Sanzen-in attracts huge crowds in late autumn when the maples peak; an early morning or late afternoon visit is advised.*

Jakko-in

Kamakura Period

· ·

The bell tower beside the pond catches the sun's last rays.

On 25 April 1185 Minamoto warriors led by Minamoto Yoshitsune defeated Taira forces at sea at Dan-no-ura in the western end of Honshu, and so brought to bloody conclusion a long struggle for supremacy between the two clans. The victors went on to rule the country from Kamakura under the leadership of Minamoto Yoritomo. All on the Taira side died in battle except Kenreimon-in, widow of Emperor Takakura and mother of the child Emperor Antoku, who drowned in the arms of his grandmother. Kenreimon-in was allowed to return to Kyoto, where she became a nun. She spent the last five years of her life in seclusion at Jakko-in.

According to temple information, Prince Shotoku founded Jakko-in in 594, but this attribution is unconfirmed and buildings date from the Kamakura period with subsequent restorations. A long flight of rustic, tree-lined steps leads to a simple entrance gate and the front garden, where a pond shaped like the ideogram for heart lies left of the *hondo* in the shelter of an old pine tree. The secluded main rear garden nestles against a densely forested hillside. Here a waterfall steps down through trees on the lower slopes ahead of rapids that flow under a bridge into a small, open pond edged with rocks and clipped azaleas. Forest trees on hillsides surround the grounds, merging with mature garden plants and trees to create continuity and enclosure.

Some observers talk of a melancholy mood, as if Kenreimon-in's sad history is made visible. On this we can not comment – we first saw Jakko-in in romantic circumstances, deep in winter snow, then again when new construction works and autumn crowds disturbed its rustic solitude.

K2 *From the Ohara terminal walk along a path running west downhill into and then along a valley running in a north-west direction.*

Rengeji

Edo period

. . . .

Rengeji's intimate pond garden lies behind the *shoin* at the foot of a very steep and luxuriantly wooded hillside. Banks are composed of tightly integrated rocks, clipped bushes and moss, all overhung with maple tracery. Lanterns, in some seasons barely glimpsed through foliage, and a stone bridge provide incidental centres of interest. A rock turtle island, with an azalea on its back, lies close to the right-hand shore. Timber walkways lead off to the right,

Autumn foliage almost conceals the lantern.

allowing visitors to walk into the garden and view the *shoin* across the pond. An illusion of spaciousness is created through a diversity of delicate and harmoniously scaled details, and in the way the pond mirrors the background foliage – lively with the lime-green of young maple leaves in early spring and a crimson blaze in autumn.

K3 *One of the quieter gardens in Kyoto, highly recommended for contemplative viewing of Japanese garden artistry. Visit Rengeji via the Eizan Line electric railway: get off at Miyakehachiman Station, then cross the river and turn right.*

Shugakuin Imperial Villa

Edo Period

. . . .

Retired Emperor Gomizuno-o (reigned 1611–1629) chose hillside land formerly occupied by a burned-down, never-rebuilt Heian temple named Shugakuji as the location of a private retreat after his abdication. There, between 1655 and 1659, he built three villas at different levels among terraced rice fields. The retired emperor – a noted aesthete – is thought to have designed the gardens himself, probably influenced by the late Kobori Enshu, who had earlier designed gardens for his principal residence, the Sento Gosho.

A guided tour of the 54.5-hectare (133-acre) estate takes in the Lower and Middle Villas, each with elegant pavilions and intimate pond gardens, then climbs the path to the Upper Villa. From this path you can see, across rice fields to the left, a gigantic tiered hedge of many varieties of clipped shrubs pierced here and there by mature trees. This magnificent example of o-karikomi covers the dam wall over 200 metres (660 feet) long to the upper garden pond. The final ascent, up a flight of steps between high hedges, reaches a small plateau, site of Rinuntei (Pavilion of Near-Cloud). Immediately below lies Yokuryu-chi, the large Pond of the Bathing Dragon, contained by its tree-topped embankment. From the foreground, foliage stretches onwards in a seamless continuum to nearby wooded foothills which frame a vista of layered blue-grey mountain ranges extending to a far-away skyline. The garden's boundaries cannot be defined, and the entire, vast space becomes a single entity under the unifying sky. This is the most spectacular example of *shakkei* in Japan.

From Rinuntei more steps descend to a bridge and the path around the pond. At first this path seems like some forest trail, then the mirror of the water is seen through the trees; islands and bridges appear, disappear and reappear in an orchestrated sequence of views as you pass around finally to the west shore. From here, to the east, there is a vision of the Chitose-bashi (Bridge of a Thousand Years) against a backdrop of luxuriantly wooded mountainside while, to the west, lie views of Kyoto over the magnificent hedge.

K4 *Book tours of Shugakuin some days ahead with passport at the Imperial Household Agency in Kyoto or Tokyo. Although only an hour long and carefully controlled, the tour is relatively relaxed and highly recommended. Take either the Eizan Railway to Shugakuin station or bus 5 to Shugakuin-rikyu-michi. Turn right at the street off Shirakawa-dori alongside the canal – Shugakuin is about 15 minutes walk ahead.*

The wonderful sweep of lake and garden seen from Rinuntei.

Manshu-in

Edo Period

· ·

Manshu-in is a Monzeki temple, one whose abbot is always a member of the imperial family. Prince Ryosho (1622–1693), second son of Prince Toshihito who built the Old Shoin at Katsura, moved Manshu-in from an earlier location north of the Imperial Palace to its present site when he was abbot in 1656. The imperial family's refined tastes are seen in two outstanding examples of *sukiya*-style architecture – the Greater Shoin (Daishoin) and, particularly, the Lesser Shoin (Shoshoin). Both face the garden.

From the Lesser Shoin, we gaze over the *karesansui* garden towards the waterfall rock.

The *karesansui* garden's background landscape includes an artificial mountain with a Mt Horai rock formation on the left-hand side. A waterfall rock towers above a stream which flows under a bridge, around a rock island and into a sea surrounding two islands. One, a crane island connected to a peninsula by a stone bridge, carries a four-hundred-year-old pine tree shaped to suggest the body and wings of a crane. The other is a turtle island. Trees behind the garden merge with hillside forests, providing a soft green envelope for the symbolic landforms.

K5 *Manshu-in is located in quiet north-eastern foothills not far from the imperial villa of Shugakuin. The nearest bus is about 15 minutes' walk. Take bus 5 from Kyoto station and get off at Shugakuin-rikyu-michi. Or take Eizan railway to Shugakuin station.*

Shisendo

Edo Period

. . . .

shikawa Jozan (1583–1672), the creator of Shisendo, abandoned his career as a brave if impetuous warrior serving Tokugawa Ieyasu for a life of poetry and scholarship in Kyoto at the age of thirty-three. This ambition was delayed by the need to work in a provincial city in a minor position to support his ailing mother. She died in 1635, and he was fifty-eight when he built Shisendo. By then an accomplished calligrapher and poet, he hung portraits of thirty-six famous Chinese poets around the walls of his study, built a garden in the so-called 'literary man's style'* and lived the last thirty years of his life there in semi-seclusion.

No photograph seen nor description read quite prepares you for the explosion of light and colour that greets you as you first gaze on Shisendo's garden; the emotional impact in certain lights and seasons can be overwhelming. The approach begins quietly up shady rustic stone steps from the street, then, by-passing the entrance court, through the dark interior past the Hall of Poetry Immortals to the verandah where the bright white sand and clustered azalea bushes of the upper garden spread before you. Luxuriant maples clothing an adjoining hillside counterpoint the azaleas' precisely rounded forms and flame a complementary golden-red in autumn; in

Spring

Summer

· ·

Autumn

Winter

spring the azaleas are clipped to maintain their shapes while still allowing delicate trails of pink buds to open. Below, but not visible from the building, is another garden where a water-fed bamboo 'deer-scarer' emits regular loud clacking noises.

The 'literary man's style' rejects the canons of taste and composition prevailing during the Tokugawa regime in favour of a more personal and idiosyncratic expression.

K6 *Sadly, age and natural calamity has caused removal of the fine sasanqua tree that shaded and cast its flowers upon the sand plane for so many years. We understand an appropriate replacement is sought. Shisendo is in the north-east foothills. Take bus 5 from the station and get off at Ichijoji Sagarimatsu-cho. Shisendo is a few minutes' stroll up the hill. Or take the Eizan railway to Ichijoji – a longer walk.*

Ginkakuji (Silver Pavilion)

Muromachi Period

· ·

Ashikaga Yoshimasa (1436–1490), the eighth Ashikaga shogun, was an aesthete and patron of the arts, but also an indifferent governor. Political stability, already vulnerable when he assumed office at the age of thirteen, disintegrated during his stewardship until Kyoto was eventually reduced to ashes by the Onin War (1467–1477). Among burned and looted palaces and temples was Saihoji, whose garden the shogun admired, often visited, and sought to emulate when he commenced building his palatial retirement villa in the lower slopes of Higashiyama in 1482. The villa was converted to the Zen temple Jishoji as a memorial to Yoshimasa after his death.

Two buildings, the Togudo and the Ginkaku (Silver Pavilion), and the garden although altered, have survived subsequent vicissitudes. The Togudo hall is an important early prototype of *shoin*-style architecture and contains a four-and-a-half-mat room thought to be a model for later tea rooms. By popular account, Yoshimasa intended to cover part

The Silver Sand Sea and the cone of the Moon Facing Height.

. . . .

Across the pond, the dark timbers of the Silver Pavilion.

of the two-storey pavilion with silver in a mark of respect for his grandfather Yoshimitsu, who had earlier built a gold-covered ceiling in Kinkakuji.

Ginkakuji's gardens are on two levels. The upper hillside garden includes a rock-embellished spring resembling an earlier construction at Saihoji and the remains of a *karedaki*. The original lower garden remains best preserved in and around the pond area facing the Togudo, but the entire pond garden has a lyrical loveliness abruptly counterpointed by a stark raised bed of white sand known as the Silver Sand Sea. The Moon Facing Height, a truncated sand cone, stands nearby. These sculptural piles may have been later additions, or result from the incremental amplification of a sand plane and a reserve mound over many years. To some eyes they are intrusive, others find the uncompromised conjunction of abstract and natural forms exhilarating.

The gardens' design, sometimes attributed to Soami, is believed by a body of scholars to have resulted from collaboration between Yoshimasa and Zen'ami, the renowned *kawaramono* who died in 1483, and to have been executed by Zen'ami's successors.

K7 *Ginkakuji lies east of Shirakawa-dori. Take bus 5 from Kyoto station and get off at Ginkakuji-michi. Ginkakuji is often crowded so early arrival is recommended.*

EAST OF THE TAKANO & KAMO RIVERS

Hakusasonso

Taisho/Showa Periods

· ·

Hakusasonso

Artist Hashimoto Kansetsu (1883–1945) created the Hakusasonso stroll garden over many years around the studio and villa he built in 1916.

A spacious pond east of the studio narrows at its southern end and then widens into a more intimate and irregular spread of water between a tea house and a small pavilion. The eastern section of the garden is elaborated with gates, bridges, stepping stones, lanterns and pagodas, and overhung with maples that have a glorious presence in late November. The western section, more open in character, is dotted with small stone figures among moss beds, rocks and trees. Kansetsu's paintings are displayed in a gallery near the garden's exit.

K8 *Hakusasonso lies a few minutes west of Ginkakuji. Opens 10.00. Also not far from Ginkakuji is the temple of* **Honen-in**, *established in 1680 in honour of Honen, founder of the Jodo Sect of Buddhism. Although the temple's interior garden is usually closed to the public, beautiful random stone walkways and gardens outside justify a visit. The most remarkable feature is a pair of rectangular sand piles at the foot of the thatch-roofed gate, their surfaces raked into decorative seasonal motifs or abstract representations of natural phenomena.*

Honen-in

Heian Shrine

Meiji Period

Bridge foundation piers form the famous stepping stones.

Kyoto commemorated eleven hundred years of existence by building and consecrating in 1895 the Heian Shrine, a prominent vermilion-coloured landmark in the north-east quarter of the city. The building, designed as a reduced-scale version of the Chodo-in (Hall of State) of the old Imperial Palace, embraces a gravel forecourt entered from the south. Gardens are laid out around the west, north and east sides.

Designed by Ogawa Jihei, the gardens pay homage to the Heian period in their emphasis on ponds and in the presence of a Chinese-style covered bridge, the Taiheikaku. They are otherwise regarded as representing Meiji period trends in plant selection, and have the circulation characteristics of a stroll garden. They are renowned for seasonal displays – cherry blossom, azaleas, irises, water lilies, autumn foliage – and a famous sequence of recycled pier stones, used as stepping stones through the north-east pond.

K9 *The Heian Shrine lies south of Marutamachi-dori, a little to the east of Higashioji-dori. Bus 5 runs from Kyoto station to near the south entrance or you can walk from Higashiyama station on the Tozai line. A little further south is the Kyoto National Museum of Modern Art, an elegant building designed by Maki Fumihiko, one of Japan's finest modern architects.*

GARDENS AT NANZENJI

K10–K13

· ·

Nanzenji is the headquarters of the Zenshu Sect of Rinzai Zen Buddhism. It occupies land where Emperor Kameyama, who reigned from 1259 to 1274, built his retirement palace. The palace was converted to a temple in 1291 under the leadership of the Zen Buddhist priest Mukan Fumon. Most buildings were destroyed during the Onin War (1467–1477).

Tokugawa Ieyasu initiated a program of assistance to Kyoto's temples and appointed a former follower turned monk named Suden to be his administrator. Suden used the sub-temple Konchi-in as his headquarters. Nanzenji benefited from Tokugawa assistance in 1611 when the Seiryoden, a National Treasure, was transferred from the Imperial Palace to serve as the abbot's 'Greater' Hojo.

The 'Lesser' Hojo, moved from Hideyoshi's Fushimi Castle and also a National Treasure, is located north of the Seiryoden. Both halls have Kano-school paintings, some attributed to Kano Eitoku (1543-1590), the school's acknowledged master.

A massive two-storey gate, Sanmon, dominates the western end of Nanzenji's grounds, an open park-like space popular in autumn.

Nanzenji is located in the eastern foothills. Take bus 5 from the station and get off at Eikando-mae, or take the subway and get off at Keage station on the Tozai line.

EAST OF THE TAKANO & KAMO RIVERS

Nanzenji Hojo

Edo Period

. . . .

The main garden lies in a walled space south of the Seiryoden. A field of white raked sand abutting the verandah occupies most of the space, while an area towards the back contains carefully integrated rocks, plants and moss. Sometimes called the Leaping Tiger Garden, it has however no obvious symbolism; rocks seem to be chosen and located on aesthetic grounds. A parallel relationship is evident between the way the rocks are massed (larger towards the rear and to the left), and the massing beyond of garden wall, temple roofs and hillside. This connection, aided by colour consistency between rocks and roofs, and between sand and walls ties the garden and its background into a beautifully balanced and unified composition.

K10 *The Hojo is located at the eastern end of Nanzenji precinct.*

Hazy sun across the Hojo's garden on a cool autumn day. The largest rock echoes the profile of the background mountain.

Nanzen-in

Kamakura Period (Edo reconstructions)

. . . .

Originally part of retired Emperor Kameyama's villa, Nanzen-in's leafy pond and stroll garden owes its present attractive state to recent renovations following a history of alterations and long periods of neglect since the Onin War.

The *hojo* overlooks ponds on its south and west sides, the more interesting aspect being southerly where the pond lies beyond narrow mossy banks carrying low, clipped bushes and rocks. A fine *horai* rock on an island provides the garden's principle focal point, a small *kamejima* lying west adds further interest, while

Vivid colour contrasts illuminate the pond at Nanzen-in.

a double-step waterfall on the far side, partly hidden by foliage, brings depth and mystery to the eastern end. A path around the pond leads off into the shady background.

K11 *While probably too much altered to possess historic significance, Nanzen-in is worth seeing for its picturesque qualities, particularly in autumn. The temple is south of the Nanzenji Hojo, and approached under the aqueduct.*

Tenju-an

Kamakura Period (Edo alterations)

. . . .

The fourteenth-century path of diagonally placed stepping stones.

Tenju-an was constructed in 1337 to commemorate the founding of Nanzenji by Mukan Fumon. Destroyed in the Onin War, it was rebuilt in 1602 with financial assistance from daimyo Hosokawa Yusai. There are two gardens; a *karesansui* garden east of the main hall and a pond garden to the south.

The white, raked gravel bed in the *karesansui* garden is split by a moss-edged path of diagonally set squared stepping stones. Connecting the main gate to the main hall, this path is said to have been constructed in 1338 soon after the temple was built. Another shorter path leading to Yusai's mausoleum was made after his death in 1610. The pond, in its charmingly overgrown garden, has eastern and western sections on either side of two opposing peninsulas. Some details, such as islands and the rock arrangement near the waterfall, are said to indicate fourteenth-century construction although the garden has been remodelled on several occasions.

K12 *Tenju-an is on the western side of the Nanzenji precinct.*

EAST OF THE TAKANO & KAMO RIVERS

Konchi-in

Edo Period

. . . .

Suden commissioned master garden-designer Kobori Enshu to build the *karesansui* garden south of the *hojo*. Construction was completed in 1632. As the garden is one of a very small number authoritatively attributed to Enshu, it has historic as well aesthetic significance.

A rectangular sand plane, raked into a tight wave pattern and empty apart from a curving path of stepping stones in one corner, is backed by a wall of clipped bushes. Centrally, at the foot of the bank, there is a large *zazenseki*. A rock composition in a cleft behind the prayer stone suggests a mountain gorge falling away from a distant waterfall. A turtle island, with its head pointing left (some experts say right) and bearing a wonderfully

Konchi-in is an eternal challenge to photograph. The *tsurujima* from within the temple.

windswept cypress, lies on the left-hand side of the sand plane. A crane island on the right directs the long expressive rock that is its head towards the turtle. While the garden is balanced and resolved as an whole, each of these three groupings can be viewed as an independent pictorial composition, framed by openings in the *hojo's* external shoji.

Approaching the *hojo* you pass by a small garden formed around a pond set out in the shape of the ideogram for heart. Of later construction, this garden forms part of a circulation system that allows visitors to climb the bank and walk behind Enshu's garden to the Toshogu Shrine dedicated to the spirit of Nanzenji's benefactor, Tokugawa Ieyasu.

K13 *Konchi-in, one of Kyoto's treasures, is mercifully free from visitor pressures often encountered in Kyoto gardens. It is not far along a narrow street that runs south just before the entrance to Nanzenji temple complex.*

Murin-an

Meiji Period

Lyrical water reflections: looking towards the main building.

The sights and sounds of water enliven Murin-an's open meadow-like garden at the foot of Higashiyama.

The land rises gently in a triangular tree-enclosed space to an apex at the far end where a three-step waterfall marks the water's entry. Water then flows from a small pool below the falls, through rapids into a broad, shallow pond dotted with stones. Here the surface is moving very slowly and reflections of overhead trees are broken, the shapes clear but slightly distorted like drawings done with a shaky hand.

The stream narrows to a shallow waterfall and then spreads into a languid, deeper pond with perfect reflections. Now the journey becomes a succession of rivulets, rapids, falls and pools until, after being joined by another stream from the other side, it exits under a corridor bridge structure. Occasional clipped bushes and rocks punctuate the grassy spaces between the streams. Surrounding trees part near the apex to borrow the scenery of nearby Higashiyama.

Yamagata Aritomo, a Meiji/Taisho period statesman, built Murin-an between 1894 and 1896 on land formerly owned by Nanzenji. The garden results from collaboration between Aritomo and Ogawa Jihei who also made the gardens at the Heian shrine. It was donated to the city in 1941.

K14 *Murin-an is near Nanzenji. Take bus 5 from Kyoto station, get off at Jingu-michi. Otherwise take the subway to Keage station on the Tozai line.*

EAST OF THE TAKANO & KAMO RIVERS

Kodaiji

Edo Period

. . . .

Kita no Mandokoro, widow of Toyotomi Hideyoshi, established Kodaiji in 1605 to honour her late husband. Tokugawa Ieyasu extensively financed construction of the temple (then known as Kodaiseiju Zenji), and the resulting buildings were renowned for their beauty and craftsmanship. Only five structures survived fires late in the eighteenth century: two tea houses designed by Sen no Rikyu for Hideyoshi's Fushimi Castle in southern Kyoto and moved to their present location, Kaisando (Founder's Hall), Kangetsudai (Moon Viewing Stage) and Otama-ya, the Sanctuary. All these buildings are Important Cultural Properties.

Legend says Kobori Enshu designed the garden over one already existing. A pond lying west of Kaisando is divided into two sections by a bridge called Rosenro, or Tower Boat Way: the larger northern section containing a *kamejima*, and the southern part a *tsurujima*. The tea houses, Kasatei (Umbrella Pavilion) and Shiguretei (Autumn Shower Pavilion), are connected by a corridor and located on a rise at the back of the site where, exquisite as they are, they have no bearing on the rest of the garden. Kyoto's eastern hills are incorporated as borrowed scenery, giving the garden a spatial depth far exceeding its material limits. Kodaiji's garden has been designated a Place of Historical Importance and Outstanding Scenery.

K15 *Kodaiji is located in the foothills east of Gion. Take bus 206 from the station and get off at Higashiyama-Yasui.*

Looking beyond Kangetsudai, in the bridge, to Kaisando.

Chishaku-in

Edo Period

Diminishing perspective of the stream vanishing south.

Toyotomi Hideyoshi built a temple called Shounji on the site now occupied by Chishaku-in in memory of his son Sutemaru, who died in 1591 aged three. After Hideyoshi's death, Tokugawa Ieyasu handed Shounji to the priests of Chishaku-in whose earlier temple in Kii province (Wakayama prefecture) had been destroyed by Hideyoshi's forces in 1585. The present garden dates from 1674, when the temple was rebuilt. In an unusual feature, thought by some to result from a later alteration, the *shoin's* verandah overlaps the pond in the manner of a *tsuridono* (fishing pavilion).

From normal viewing positions the pond's furthermost limits can not be seen. The garden is said to be inspired by the mountain of Lu-shan in China, and the pond resembles part of some endless river winding its way through a mountainous terrain. Scale and perspective are manipulated to create an illusion of deep space in the southern section. The slender proportions of a three-piece bridge near the tea room enhance the pond's apparent width, while beyond this the pond and its flanks are tapered to exaggerate perspective depth. A lantern just visible above shrubbery on the far eastern slope is diminished in appearance as if seen far away.

The waterfall that tumbles down through bushes and rocks covering the steep hillside facing the *shoin* provides the garden's focal point. Originally dry, this waterfall now contains a tiny stream that splashes gently into the pond over a grooved rock.

K16 *Chishaku-in is on the eastern side of the T-junction formed by Shichijo-dori and Higashioji-dori and is well served by buses in both streets. Admission includes access to a museum displaying paintings originally in Shounji.*

Detail of the waterfall entering the pond.

GARDENS AT TOFUKUJI

K17–K19

. . . .

Tofukuji, in its prime one of the Gozan (literally Five Mountains), the five most prominent Zen temples in Kyoto, has suffered extensive damage from warfare and fires since it was founded in 1236. Buildings in today's smaller precinct date from the Muromachi period.

Take the JR Nara Line to Tofukuji station or bus 208 from Kyoto station. Also accessible from Tofukuji station on Keihan Railway.

Fumon-in (Kaisando)

Edo Period

. . . .

The garden at Fumon-in, a sub-temple of Tofukuji, lies between a two-storey entrance gate and the Founder's Hall (Kaisando) and is thought to have been built about the middle of the seventeenth century.

A stone path splits the garden into two parts of very different character. To the west is a flat sand plane raked into a checker-board pattern with three different textures and containing, in one corner, a group of rocks and shrubs forming a crane island. A narrow pond edged with rocks and small clipped shrubs, crossed by finely scaled stone bridges, runs alongside the path on the eastern side. Beyond the pond, clipped bushes and occasional rocks extend up a hillside to a crowning band of mature trees.

The path was added to the original garden and early twentieth-century photographs show a freely planted eastern hillside which seems to have dramatised, through contrast, the carefully crafted western side. The present garden appears more open, uniting landscape elements with the architectural components of gate, hall and linking colonnades in a clearly defined and handsome space.

The unusual sand pattern appears to have inspired modern gardens at the nearby Hojo, where a temple reference alludes to a Chinese way of dividing land. From this, it can be inferred that the Fumon-in pattern symbolises the 'well-field system', an idealised way of arranging agricultural land that came into being some time before the Han dynasty (206 BC–AD 220). The system grouped square fields in blocks of nine, three fields each side with a common well in the centre, and the arrangement was held to generate cooperation, self-sufficiency and social stability in agricultural communities.

K17 *One of the quieter gardens in Kyoto. Entry tickets are purchased at the entry to Tsuten-kyo (Bridge to Heaven), famous for viewing autumn foliage in the valley it crosses.*

Fumon-in's square-raked sand.

Tofukuji Hojo

Showa Period

. . . .

Shigemori Mirei designed four *karesansui* gardens for the Hojo in 1938. They are said by the temple 'to express the simplicity of Zen in the Kamakura period with the abstract construction of modern arts'.

The south garden shows four rock groups symbolising isles of the immortals, in a sea of raked gravel known as Hakkai (Eight Rough Seas). Bold, ruggedly textured vertical or angular shapes generally characterise these rocks, counterpointed by some massive horizontals. Five moss-covered mounds in the western end provide complementary rounded forms and refer to the temple's early status. Another marriage of opposing elements is seen again in the west garden, where a wavy-edged moss bed meets a grid symbolising Chinese land division in alternating gravel

squares and low azalea hedges. The grid, which also seems to reflect the checker-board sand pattern in the older nearby garden at Fumon-in, is carried into the north garden's pattern of squared stones set in a moss matrix. The settings become more random towards the free-form east garden, where seven old foundation stones are arranged to represent the stars of the Great Bear.

K18 *Tofukuji Hojo is situated at the northern edge of the main complex, bordering the maple valley.*

Yin/yang: soft mossy curves meet a grid of azaleas and sand.

Sesshuji (Funda-in)

Muromachi Period

· ·

Sesshu Toyo is believed to have designed Sesshuji's garden about 1465; the temple now bears his name. The temple, originally known as Funda-in, had been built about 1321 by Ichijo Uchitsune with Jozan Sozen as founding priest. It remained the Ichijo family temple, and Ichijo Kanera had Sesshu lay out the garden while staying at the temple during his time in Kyoto. Shigemori Mirei renovated the neglected garden in 1939.

The main rock groupings set in a mossy sward. Delicate touches within the *engawa* at Sesshuji are the shoji opening pulls, with pressed leaves set in handmade paper.

The garden wraps around the south and east sides of the *hojo*. A spread of raked, white sand lies alongside the southern verandah, and beyond is a sweep of moss in which stand two rock groupings: a turtle island to the west and a crane island to the east. The turtle island is built with rocks at two levels, with its head on the left. The dominant rocks in the crane island have that flat-topped angularity associated with Sesshu's work. The east garden consists of a moss bed with small rock settings that represent *horai* mountains, and turtle and crane islets. Both sections are contained by clipped hedges, and there is a fine group of bushes topiarised into semi-spherical or squarish shapes at their junction. The south garden is backed by a wall of foliage including camellias, and a bamboo grove.

K19 *From Tofukuji station walk south along the road east of the railway line, take the second road on the left, and the entrance to Sesshuji is on the south side of this road, about mid-block.*

Kajuji

Heian Period

· ·

The *horai* island and pond seen from a trellised rest spot covered with wisteria.

*E*mperor Daigo founded the temple of Kajuji in 900 on the site of a ninth-century residence built by Fujiwara Miyamichi. Kajuji's garden surrounds a large pond named Himuro-no-ike and designed to be enjoyed while boating. The temple tells that Himuro-no-ike had special significance during the Heian period, when ice on its surface was dedicated to the imperial court on the second day in January every year and, from the ice's thickness, the success of the forthcoming grain harvest would be divined.

Views of the garden from the temple side show a composition in four complementary layers: foreground planting and details, the pond's bushy *horai* island, trees behind the pond and, framed by trees in the distance, the borrowed scenery of a softly rounded mountain summit. These views are rich in vegetation but contain few rocks and no structures, so much of the garden now appears a natural setting rather than an artifice.

K20 *Kajuji can most easily be reached on the subway, getting off at Ono on the Tozai line.*

Jonangu Shrine

Showa Period

. . . .

Grasses curve against white gravel like the formalised gold clouds in traditional paintings. A cherry tree bared by autumn reveals its great supporting trellises.

The Jonangu Shrine's gardens were designed by Nakane Kinsaku with the assistance of botanist Dr Hiroe Minosuke. Over one hundred plants depicted in *The Tale of Genji* are said to be planted, giving rise to its description as The Garden of Flowers of *The Tale of Genji*. The site was once part of the retirement villa of Emperor Shirakawa (reigned 1072–1086).

There are actually five gardens in different styles covering a total area of 2 hectares (5 acres). The usual route leads through an entrance garden called Spring Hill, then along a leafy meandering path around the back of the shrine building to the Heian Style Garden, where a pond with an island, a small hill and a waterfall form a natural-looking arrangement. A winding stream is the twice-yearly scene of poetry parties. Across a driveway, on the north side of a tea house, the Muromachi Style Garden is built around a long narrow pond edged with rock groups and trimmed plants, and bisected by a bridge. The Momoyama Style Garden, a *karesansui* garden with the usual sand replaced by lawn, lies south of the tea house. In this stylish composition, a tall clipped background hedge represents a mountain range; clusters of rocks and plants (cycads in one dramatic instance) symbolise islands.

The final garden, featuring undulating beds of ground cover studded with rocks said to symbolise buildings that stood in the Jonan Imperial Villa some eight hundred years ago, looks modern. At this point you can see how the sequence of gardens has been orchestrated to become more abstracted as the journey through them proceeds, and how these elegantly detailed, impeccably maintained gardens ultimately transcend the limitations of recreating period styles.

K22 *Jonangu Shrine is an entertaining 20 minutes' walk south and west from Takeda subway station, through architectural fantasies in Kyoto's love hotel district.*

Byodo-in

Uji • Heian Period

. . . .

Morning at the sublime Phoenix Hall.

The Phoenix Hall at Byodo-in, beautifully reflected in the calm waters of the Aji pond, has somehow defied warfare, fires, earthquakes and the ordinary ravages of time to offer a glimpse of Heian-period splendour.

Emperors and aristocrats built villas in the picturesque Uji area during the Heian period, Fujiwara Michinaga (966–1027), *kampaku* or chief adviser to the emperor and the most powerful man in the land, among them. His son Yorimichi (990–1072) converted the villa into a temple named Byodo-in in 1052, and in 1053 had the chapel now known as the Phoenix Hall (or Ho-o-do) dedicated to Amida Buddha. Further buildings were added over the next two decades until, at the time of Yorimichi's death, some thirty-three buildings including seven pagodas complemented his grand recreation of Amida's Western Paradise.

The Phoenix Hall, so named for the imagery of its flanking wing-like arcades and the aerodynamic lightness of its structure, is the only surviving original building. The central hall houses a 3-metre (10-feet) high gilded statue of Amida Buddha resting on a lotus pedestal under an elaborate canopy inlaid with mother-of-pearl, and fifty-two carved *bodhisattvas* floating on clouds around its upper levels, all National Treasures. Wall and door murals depict Amida Buddha and attendants welcoming the spirits of believers into the Western Paradise over four seasons. Only the central hall is enclosed; the remainder of the building is fundamentally ornamental, and pavilions on the ends of the wings resemble the fishing pavilions of *shinden* mansions.

K23 *Uji is reached most directly on the Keihan Uji line. At Uji cross the bridge over the river, and turn left through the arch with the two phoenixes into the street leading to Byodo-in. Or take the JR line from Kyoto station, and walk down the main street to the river, turn right at the phoenixes.*

Garden of Fine Art

Heisei Period

. . . .

The Garden of Fine Art continues the vein of abstraction first introduced in Ryoanji to a level where definitions of what constitutes a garden become questioned. Water apart, there is nothing here in a natural state unless framed views of trees in the adjoining Botanic Gardens are included.

The 'garden' is housed within a roofless, sculptural, concrete structure on several levels designed by Ando Tadao, who also designed Honpukuji on Awajishima. On display are ceramic reproductions of painting

Waterfalls, glass balustrades and full-scale ceramic reproductions form a stroll garden where focal points are paintings.

masterpieces, both western and oriental, that are claimed to be colour accurate and long lasting. They are mounted in steel frames against, or recessed into, smooth concrete walls, except in one case: Monet's *Water Lilies - Morning*, viewed full size under water. Works by Renoir and Van Gogh and two scroll paintings are seen at four times their original size. *Sunday Afternoon on the Island of La Grande Jatte* by Seurat and Leonardo da Vinci's *The Last Supper* are presented in full size, as is the garden's climactic work, Michelangelo's *The Last Judgement* from the Sistine Chapel.

K25 *Near the Kitayama subway station in north Kyoto; leave the station by exit 3. Closed 28 Dec–Jan.*

GARDENS AT DAITOKUJI

K26–K31

. . . .

Daito Kokushi (1282–1337) founded Daitokuji as a Rinzai Zen temple in 1319. He converted emperors Hanazono and Godaigo (combined reign 1308–1339) to the discipline, and with imperial patronage the temple prospered until successive disasters of fire in 1453 and war in 1468 led to its destruction. The priest Ikkyu (1394–1481) commenced reconstruction in 1474 with support from Emperor Gotsuchimikado (reigned 1465–1500). Most sub-temples were built in the sixteenth century when Daitokuji was patronised by aristocrats and warriors who were also tea ceremony devotees. Ikkyu is thought to have instructed his student Shuko in tea practices imported from China. Shuko, in turn, organised them into a formal ceremony with spiritual significance, and so came about a symbiotic relationship between Zen, the tea ceremony, priests and their high-placed students that saw Daitokuji grow in stature as a temple particularly associated with the tea ceremony. Sen no Rikyu (1522–1591), most famous of all tea masters, took instructions from Shorei Sokin, the founder of the sub-temple Juko-in.

Juko-in opens to the public for short winter seasons but photography is not permitted. Built in 1566, it has doors (National Treasures) painted by Kano-school artists and a *karesansui* garden depicting a lake and some islands. This gentle composition of mossy plane, rocks, stone bridge and a hedge clipped to symbolise mountains is further described in Chapter 2. The sub-temple Koho-an has similar restrictions. Kobori Enshu created *karesansui* gardens there c 1621 as landscapes that might be observed from a boat. Seated viewers in the Bosen tea room see, below a half-raised vertically sliding shoji, a 'shore' of dark grey pebbles, a lantern and a basin. This famous intimate scene flows around one side of a short hedge into a panorama of lake and landforms. In a sea of moss (covered in winter with pine needles) seen from the *hojo* a mound with small pines suggests an island, while a double stepped hedge implies waves.

Daitokuji is on the north side of Kitaoji-dori west of Kitaoji station, about 15 minutes' walk. Buses 205, 206 connect Daitokuji with Kyoto railway station. **K26** *Juko-in is at the north-west corner of the intersection of Daitokuji's main paths.* **K27** *Koho-an is a little west of the main compound.*

Daisen-in

Muromachi Period

. . . .

Kogaku Soko, founder of Daisen-in in 1509, built its *karesansui* garden after completing the main hall in 1513, possibly assisted by Soami, who painted door panels. A narrow L-shaped area around the north-east corner of the *shoin* contains a three-dimensional evocation of a Northern Sung-style landscape painting, represented through some of the most beautiful and expressive rocks to be seen in Japan.

Softly filtered light and snow ripples: one of the south garden's sand cones.

The scene is some vast mountainous landscape. A rock with off-white vertical striations represents a distant waterfall at the head of a torrent that spills down into lower falls past towering crags, spreading into two branches. The west flows past a turtle island into the 'middle sea', while the other streams under a stone bridge, past a crane island and other rocks into the east side of the garden. It moves under a covered walkway into an area where a boat rock sails towards a *horai* rock island.

The graphic nature to the east contrasts with the minimalism of the south garden. Here, a rectangular plane of white gravel is empty apart from two small gravel cones and a corner Bodhi tree. This may be seen as the sea at the end of the river's journey, an essay in balance, a canvas for passing decorations applied by shadows or snow-drifts, or metaphorically, the serenity attainable through meditation.

K28 *Daisen-in is in the northern part of Daitokuji.*

Zuiho-in

Showa Period

Shigemori's influence exceptionally well-realised in the typically forceful use of dynamic rocks and deeply furrowed sand rakings.

Otomo Sorin, heir of a daimyo in Kyushu, dedicated Zuiho-in to the 91st patriarch of Daitokuji in 1546. Otomo later converted to Christianity. The temple pamphlet describes him as a ruthless war-lord who exploited his faith politically. Two *karesansui* gardens built in the 1960s commemorate the dual nature of his religious affiliations, and manifest on-going compassion for the temple's founder.

The south garden depicts the towering peaks of a *horai* island set in an ocean symbolised by sand raked into deep wave patterns. The composition is rugged, linear and dynamic, with a strong diagonal thrust transmitted along a peninsula to a free-standing rock near the eastern side. The ocean narrows at the western end to a tranquil inlet meandering through moss land masses.

The north garden takes a Christian theme, with a cruciform arrangement of rocks representing islands and mountains. There is also a tea garden with stepping stones and a basin set in a field of large cobble-stones.

K29 *Zuiho-in is on the west side of a small cul-de-sac running from the south-west corner of the central area of Daitokuji.*

Ryogen-in

Muromachi Period

. . . .

Ryogen-in has five gardens, the most important being Ryogintei (Dragon Singing Garden), attributed to Soami in temple literature or sometimes to Tokei Soboku, who founded the temple in 1502. Other experts believe the temple was completed after Tokei's death in 1517, and the garden built about that time. In any event, it is one of the oldest *karesansui* gardens in Japan.

Ryogintei lies in a walled space on the north side of the *hojo*. A central rock group near the back wall is dominated by a beautiful tall rock,

Once sand, now a moss sea where a standing rock represents Shumisen.

tilted to the east, and interpreted as representing Shumisen. A small, delicately balanced *sanzon* group lies a little to the right. The garden floor, now covered in moss, was originally entirely sand.

Isshidan, the garden south of the *hojo*, was reconstructed in 1980 as a *karesansui* composition with three rock groups: a *horaisan* in the far corner, a *tsurujima* in the right foreground, and a *kamejima* on the left. The tiny Totekiko, a *tsubo-niwa* (small enclosed garden) constructed only of rocks and raked sand in 1958, is the most interesting of the other gardens.

K30 *Ryogen-in is entered on the west side of the main north-south path in Daitokuji, just south of the central cluster of temple structures.*

Koto-in

Momoyama Period

. . . .

Autumn at Koto-in.

Hosokawa Tadaoki (1563–1645), a Momoyama-period warrior who supported in turn Oda Nobunaga, Toyotomi Hideoyoshi and Tokugawa Ieyasu as they each dominated the country, established Koto-in in 1601. Tadaoki retired in 1619 and, taking the name Sansai, became a Buddhist priest. He took instructions in tea ceremony from Sen no Rikyu, and founded the Sansai school of ceremonial tea.

The temple is approached along a stone path flanked on both sides by light-filtering maple trees. The entrance remains concealed until the last few paces, although a bell-shaped window at the end of the longest section is designed to allow a brief view of the principal garden. This garden, south of the *hojo*, is a moss-covered area, shaded by maple trees and backed by a stand of bamboos. A solitary lantern provides the focal point. There is also a tea garden that visitors can enter attached to a tea house known as Shokoken (Pine Facing Eaves). Tadaoki's tomb, marked with a lantern said to be of Korean stone and given to him by Sen no Rikyu, lies near other family tombs on the west side.

K31 *The garden at Koto-in, lovely at any time, is spectacular in late autumn when scarlet and gold maple leaves carpet the moss. It is located in the western section of Daitokuji, immediately south of the east-west axial path.*

Honpoji

Edo Period

. . . .

Hon'ami Koetsu, whose own garden can be seen at Koetsuji, is believed to have designed the garden at Honpoji, a temple established on its present site in 1587 with the patronage of Toyotomi Hideyoshi.

The temple calls the garden Mitsudomoe-no-niwa (Garden with Three Eddies), referring to the 'comma' forms of three islands that were included in its composition. In pictorial terms, a stream flows from a *karedaki* in the south-east corner, under a stone

Honpoji in autumn.

bridge and then spreads out as a pond over the greater part of the garden. A 'real' lotus pond, edged with ten cut stones and shaped like an opening flower, lies within this *karesansui* pond. Just north of the lotus pond lie two semicircular stones placed base to base; together they complete a circle and represent the Chinese ideogram for sun. Günter Nitschke points out that the axial, and oddly formal, arrangement of lotus pond and circle is to be read 'as an acronym for Nichiren, the thirteenth century reformer of Pure Land Buddhism whose name translates literally as "sun-lotus"'. Honpoji is a Nichiren Sect temple.

K32 *Honpoji is opened to the public for limited seasons during autumn and/or winter. Check with the Tourist Information Centre. Honpoji is on the east side of Horikawa-dori, south of the Shimei-dori intersection. A temple gallery displays a 10-metre (34-feet) high painting, the* Hotoke Nehanzu *(Buddha Nirvana Picture) by Hasegawa Tohaku (1539–1610), designated an Important Cultural Asset.*

Sento Gosho

Edo Period

. . . .

The Sento and Omiya palaces were built side by side for the retirement of Emperor Gomizuno-o (reigned 1611–1629) and Empress Tofukumon-in respectively. After a fire in 1854 destroyed both palaces for the sixth time, the Sento Palace was not rebuilt as no retired emperor was alive. The Omiya Palace was rebuilt for Empress Dowager Eisho, consort of Emperor Komei, and these days occasionally accommodates the imperial family, or visiting heads of state. The two gardens have been united and opened to the public.

Emperor Gomizuno-o collaborated with Kobori Enshu in the layout, but there have been so many subsequent changes that the present garden bears scant resemblance to the original design. Like Katsura, Sento Gosho employs hide and reveal techniques to unfold changing tableaux before the moving viewer, but here the feeling is more open and relaxed, with sweeping shorelines carrying the eye from one detail to another. A stone zig-zag bridge (*yatsuhashi*) carrying a wisteria trellis crosses the southern-most pond and provides the focal point for many views, but perhaps the most remarkable element is the cobble-stone beach curving around the southern end. According to legend, the stones were gathered in Odawara and sent to the emperor, individually wrapped in silk.

The wisteria-clad bridge beyond the pebble beach.

K33 *Book tours in advance at the office of the Imperial Household Agency (see K4 Shugakuin). Sento Gosho is located in the east side of Kyoto Imperial Park.*

Nijo Castle

Edo Period

. . . .

Tokugawa Ieyasu began building Nijo-jo soon after becoming overlord in 1600, completing the residential quarters in 1603. Although the shogunate moved its headquarters to Edo, Nijo-jo was retained to mark Tokugawa authority and for occasional shows of strength by Ieyasu and successive shoguns. The present palace and garden in the Ninomaru (secondary enclosure) dates from 1626 when the castle was expanded and remodelled for a visit from Emperor Gomizuno-o. Fires destroyed buildings over the next hundred-odd years and by the end of the eighteenth century not much more than the halls of Ninomaru remained. The palace was ill-used as municipal offices for thirteen years during the early days of the Meiji Restoration before being taken over by the imperial household in 1884 and restored. It functioned thereafter as a detached palace until 1939, when it was handed over to the city of Kyoto.

Nijo's majestic rock formations.

Kobori Enshu designed the garden to have a robust presence, possibly to be best enjoyed at some distance and from within buildings. It is composed around a large pond, containing a *horai* island, a turtle island to the south and a crane island to the north. There is a waterfall on the far side. Rocks are plentiful and massive, as if symbolising the shogun's power, and cycads add an exotic note. It is said that there were no trees in the garden originally, so that falling leaves would not remind the shogun of life's transitory nature.

K34 *Vast crowds visit Nijo-jo to see its fabulous interiors, creating unrewarding viewing conditions. Shoji close external openings, denying framed views of the garden. Paths around the pond are usually fairly busy with photographers and their human subjects. Even going early does not seem to help. Take the subway to Oike-dori and change to the Tozai line for Nijo-jo-mae.*

Shinsenen

Heian Period

. . . .

8am at Shinsenen: a quiet neighbourhood feeling remains where once Kyoto's first imperial garden extended.

Emperor Kammu built in Heiankyo, the capital he founded in 794, a grand, walled pleasure garden spreading over more than 13 hectares (33 acres) south of the Imperial Palace enclosure. It was called Shinsenen, or Divine Spring Garden, for the perpetual spring which fed its large lake. Banks were adorned with hills, plants, and pavilions, red-lacquered in the Chinese style and at times linked by corridors. Some were settings for contemplative pleasures like moon-viewing, others for fishing, poetry parties, banquets, wrestling matches or other amusements for the delectation of the emperor and his court.

For several centuries the palace suffered successive episodes of destruction and rebuilding, the court's political influence waned and eventually the site was abandoned. Warfare, neglect and sub-division eroded the garden until all that remained a few years ago was a small pond in a dusty public park alongside one of Kyoto's commercial streets. Today, Shinsenen is rather more picturesque, its banks massed with foliage. An island shrine is dedicated to Emperor Kammu; visitors can tread there and along a small section of bank near the street, but the rest is cut off from casual viewers.

K35 *Shinsenen lies north of Oike-dori, midway between Sembon-dori, and Horikawa-dori.*

Shoseien

Heian Period

An unexpected haven not far from the railway station, an engaging remnant linked back to Heian times.

Families picnic here; this peaceful garden on the edge of the busy commercial area around Kyoto station seems more of a public park than an object for admiration. Yet the history of Shoseien probably extends back to the Heian period, for the site fits descriptions of the Riverbank Villa built for Minamoto no Toru, Minister of the Left, about 872. Tokugawa Iemitsu granted the land to the abbot of nearby Higashi Honganji, and reconstruction attributed to Ishikawa Jozan and Kobori Enshu is said to have occurred in the Edo period.

The garden is built around a pond with two large and several small islands, the largest being connected to shores by bridges. Loraine Kuck observes that some rock groups on the islands are in 'typical Heian style'.

K37 *Shoseien is 5 minutes' walk east of Higashi Honganji. While in the area, wander along the Takase River a couple of streets further east and see a part of Kyoto that seems to retain its sense of community, sadly disappearing from many districts.*

Shodenji

Edo Period

Quiet and immaculate, Shodenji's 3–5–7 azalea groupings.

Shodenji sits on a benched hillside at the end of a long flight of rustic stone steps in heavily wooded scenery just beyond the northern outskirts of Kyoto, far enough from the tourist circuit to be tranquil at all times. It has a small *karesansui* garden consisting only of clipped azalea bushes and white gravel, dating from the early Edo period.

The garden, on the east side of the verandah, is contained within white, tile-capped walls. The azaleas grow just in front of the back wall and spread across the garden in groups of three, five and seven bushes. They increase in size and number to the right, which also is the side of the roofed gate, where trees immediately behind the wall build in height. Balancing this movement, Mt Hiei appears in the composition as borrowed scenery on the left.

Shodenji may be compared to Ryoanji, with which it shares qualities of abstraction and a 3–5–7 arrangement, and Entsuji in its use of Mt Hiei as borrowed scenery, but similarities end there. Shodenji has its own decorative–minimalist style in not using rocks, exemplifying the economic freedom afforded by *karesansui* gardens.

K39 *Take bus 1 from Kitaoji bus terminal and get off at Jinko-in-mae. Probably best seen in spring when the azaleas are in bloom.*

Koetsuji

Edo Period

. . . .

Educated in the courtly arts of the Heian age, Hon'ami Koetsu (1558–1637) was an outstanding artist and craftsman who established an artisans' colony in the Takagamine district in 1615 on land granted by Tokugawa Ieyasu. The colony's artists and craftsmen collaborated to produce works of a quality unmatched since Heian times.

The estate where Koetsu built a family chapel is now Koetsuji, a Nichiren Sect Buddhist temple approached from the street along a beautiful stone path lined with maple trees. Koetsuji's garden is best known for a bamboo lattice fence said to be designed by Koetsu himself. This gently curving fence separates the inner garden (*uchi roji*) of the Taikyo-an tea house from the rest of the garden, and consists of lashed diagonal slats with a bundled top; a design that has become known as Koetsugaki but is also referred to as Gagyugaki (Fence shaped like a Cow lying on the Ground). Several other tea houses stand in this rambling garden, and Koetsu's grave lies in one corner.

Koetsuji's bamboo fence.

Genko-an

K40 *From Kitaoji bus terminal, take bus Kita-1 to Genko-an-mae.* **Genko-an** *is also worth visiting for its gentle garden with mountainside borrowed scenery, particularly in autumn.*

Kinkakuji (Golden Pavilion)

Muromachi Period

. . . .

Serene against blue skies, Kinkakuji shines across the pond and its islands.

Yoshimitsu (1358–1408), the third Ashikaga shogun, converted a villa known as Kitayama-dono (North Hill Villa) on the slopes of Kitayama into a sumptuous estate following his retirement in 1394. Yoshimitsu invested his personal creativity and his love of art, Chinese culture, architecture and gardens in remodelling the one hundred and sixty–year-old garden and erecting new buildings. He named the estate Rokuon, or Deer Park, and willed it to be converted to a Zen temple after his death. The Golden Pavilion and the garden have survived to the present time, although the pavilion had to be rebuilt after a fire in 1950. The scene of the gilded pavilion across the calm waters of the pond is one of the most beautiful and emblematic in Japan.

A large *horai* island divides the pond into two parts. The section close to the pavilion is studded with islets and small islands including crane and turtle islands, while the waters further away are relatively empty to create the illusion of a space so deep that details can barely be seen. Fine trees, their heights manipulated to allow a glimpse of distant Mt Kinugasa, surround the pond. The garden includes a famous and early *ryumonbaku*, and a *rikushu-no-matsu* – a pine tree trained to resemble the hull and sail of a junk.

K41 *Located off Kitsuji-dori, Kinkaku–ji is one of Japan's greatest tourist drawcards and can be overwhelmingly crowded. Early arrival or an off-season visit is recommended. Take the subway from the station to Imadegawa-dori, then bus 59 to Kinkakuji-mae.*

Ryoanji

Muromachi Period

. . . .

Hosokawa Katsumoto founded Ryoanji in 1450 on grounds that had been developed as a residential estate during the Heian period. The Kyoyochi pond survives from this earlier use. Ryoanji was destroyed during the Onin War. Katsumoto's son, Masamoto, rebuilt the temple in 1488 and the stone garden in front of the *hojo* was built about 1499. The designer's identity is not known; some scholars believe

Autumn shadows across the sand garden.

the garden was created by *kawaramono*, riverbank-dwelling labourers who became the first professional garden-makers.

Ryoanji has, quite simply, the superlative Zen garden and no description or photograph here can represent its extraordinary impact. Fifteen rocks are spread across immaculately raked sand in groups of 5–2, 3–2 and 3 (composite groups with a 7–5–3 arrangement). The enclosing earthen wall – a blend of browns and ochres – dissociates the space from background trees; the only other plant life is a little moss around the rocks. These simple elements are assembled with unsurpassed mastery of space, form, texture and colour into a composition that engages the viewer's imagination, through the mystery of its own meaning, in the deeper mystery of all creation.

K42 *Ryoanji's fame attracts crowds of visitors and the verandah can become almost unbearably busy. Go early, late or off season to best appreciate the stone garden's calm profundity. Lunch time is often relatively quiet. Allow time to step aside during peaks (there are other attractive but hardly visited gardens around the* hojo *), enjoy the lulls in between and later stroll around the lovely grounds. Ryoanji is in the north-west foothills. Take bus 59 and get off at Ryoanji-michi.*

Ninnaji

Edo Period

. . . .

Emperor Uda (reigned 887–897) founded Ninnaji in 888 and became head priest on retirement. Thereafter head priests were always sons of imperial families until the tradition was discontinued after the Meiji Restoration. All structures in the original complex, which included more than sixty sub-temples, were destroyed during the Onin War. The Tokugawa family and the imperial household provided funds for a partial rebuilding program. Several present-day buildings date from this time. Ninnaji is now one of the headquarters of Shingon Sect Buddhism.

Gardens are attached to the 'palace' in the south-west corner of the precinct where all buildings, other than two tea houses, were rebuilt after a fire in 1887. A pine tree, with a striking horizontally trained limb, dominates the entry court. The spacious main garden, a 1690 modification of an earlier garden thought to have been modelled on paradise gardens, is on the rear (north-facing) side of the *shinden*. The centre-ground is filled by a pond fed by a waterfall and divided into two parts by a stone slab bridge. Between the building and the pond lies a foreground of raked sand, with some grass and clipped bushes on the pond's banks. The well-planted hillside beyond the pond frames a tea house. Apparent spatial depth is exaggerated through limiting the size of background trees and progressively narrowing the path leading to the bridge, then extended by capturing the tip of Ninnaji's pagoda above the tree tops.

K43 *Ninnaji is near Ryoanji. Bus 59 stops at Omuro-Ninnaji, before the temple gate. While not crowded compared to nearby Ryoanji, the garden's tranquillity is periodically interrupted by loud recorded descriptions of the temple's treasures.*

Off to the right, the tea house, normally the focal point of this view, was scaffolded for re-construction.

Toji-in

Kamakura Period (Showa reconstruction)

. . . .

Ashikaga Takauji established Toji-in in 1338 and the temple remained the family's place of worship over the span of fifteen Ashikaga shoguns. The gardens are popularly, but without certainty, credited to Muso Soseki, the first abbot. The old east pond, known as Shinjichi (Heart-shaped Pond) and bearing similarities to Saihoji, might have been constructed in his time but the area around Fuyochi (Lotus Pond) north of the *hojo* is thought to relate to the Edo period. Nakane Kinsaku has renovated the east pond in recent times.

The *hojo* overlooks a pond with a relatively large *horai* island to a small hill crowned by the tea house Seirentei, erected by eighth shogun Yoshimasa. Island and banks are smothered in rocks and precisely clipped bushes, often composed in clusters balancing various shapes and sizes. The east garden is a leafy rambling space with moss beds and old trees reflected in still water. Much of Toji-in's considerable charm comes from the juxtaposition of these contrasting characters in a single fluid space; it responds brilliantly to late afternoon light and looks spectacular in autumn.

In late dappled light, a myriad bushes tumble down slopes to the pond and the massive stone bridge.

K44 *Take bus 59 (or 50 from the station); get off at Ritsumeikan-daigaku-mae. Another high quality garden, it can easily be seen in conjunction with Ryoanji.*

GARDENS AT MYOSHINJI

K45 and K46

. . . .

The priest Egen founded Myoshinji in 1337 on land previously the site of a retirement villa for Emperor Hanazono (reigned 1308–1318). It was destroyed during the Onin War and rebuilt over subsequent centuries into today's complex of forty-seven sub-temples. Myoshinji is the headquarters of the Myoshinji school of Rinzai Zen Buddhism.

Take bus 26 from the station to Myoshinji-kitamon-mae bus stop for a north side entrance or JR San-in Line to Hanazono station for a south side approach.

Nakane's glamorous lower garden with its low spreading clipped bushes and watercourse.

Taizo-in

Muromachi Period

· ·

Looking towards the the waterfall in Taizo-in's intimate Muromachi garden with its clearcut rock formations.

The temple of Taizo-in at Myoshinji was reconstructed on its present site in the sixteenth century. It possesses an important *karesansui* garden from the Muromachi period and a modern one designed by Nakane Kinsaku.

The painter Kano Motonobu (1476–1559), who lived for some time at the temple, is thought to have designed the older garden. This assumption is lent credence through similarities between the garden and the Kano school of painting, which blended Chinese techniques with the indigenous style known as *yamato-e*. Taizo-in presents a landscape that may be seen as a three-dimensional re-creation of a landscape painting. In this respect it resembles the earlier Sung-painting-inspired garden at Daisen-in, but here the forms are gentler, more horizontal, showing the indigenous influence.

The Muromachi-period garden is west of the *hojo*. A waterfall emerges from deep forests in the north-west corner; its water spills down pebble 'rapids' into a lake surrounding a turtle island and flows away under a bridge in the south. Further bridges connect the island to shores, and a Mt Horai rock on the far side provides the central focal point. The modern garden, in a separate, lower part of the temple's grounds, features a watercourse, a pond and slopes covered in azaleas and occasional rocks. The stream is made progressively narrower as it nears its origins in a large mountain-shaped hedge to exaggerate its apparent depth, and detailling throughout reflects Nakane's mastery over placement and design.

K45 *Taizo-in is on the southern side of Myoshinji.*

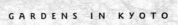

Keishun-in

Edo Period

. . . .

Stepping stones and gate to the tea garden.

*K*eishun-in was founded in 1598 and its gardens were built during the seventeenth century. They comprise a narrow *karesansui* garden south of the *hojo*, a rambling stroll garden on the south and east sides, and a tea garden.

The *karesansui* garden is defined by two clipped hedges: one low, running alongside a path at the verandah's edge; the other tall, separating the garden from background foliage. A lantern provides the focal point to the mossy space created within these hedges, which also contains some small manicured trees and a few rocks. The stroll garden, entered along a path behind the *karesansui* garden, runs downhill from the temple and has, for the most part, a leafy, overgrown, almost rustic character. Stepping stones through moss in a relatively open area near the *hojo* lead to a small gate which, in turn, opens into the tea garden off the tea room Kihaku-an.

K46 *Keishun-in is another peaceful garden outside the tourist circuit, situated in the north-east area of the Myoshinji complex.*

Osawa-no-ike (Osawa Pond)

Heian Period

. . . .

This peaceful lake enjoyed by casual strollers and picnickers, lined with maples and cherry trees, was once the centrepiece of a grand estate built for the retirement of Emperor Saga (reigned 809–823). Covering 2.5 hectares (6 acres), its survival as the most intact Heian pond is most likely due to the estate's conversion to the Buddhist temple Daikakuji in 876. Although now only a faint echo of former brilliance, Osawa-no-ike can still evoke images of those heady days when vermilion-coloured pavilions adorned its banks and dragon-headed boats carried gorgeously robed aristocrats across its mirror surface.

Late light at Osawa-no-ike.

There are two islands in the pond, the smaller one known as Kiku-no-shima (Chrysanthemum Island). A rock islet, a haven for sun-seeking turtles, lies nearby. This islet, made up of three stones, is thought to be the only survivor of five similar islets once arranged in a straight line between the two islands in a style that came to be known as 'night mooring stones' from their resemblance to a line of junks moored in some safe harbour.

A cascade of rocks built into the hillside north of the pond is now thought to have been built as a *karedaki*. This would make it the oldest one discovered in Japan and, as the garden is believed to have been modelled on contemporary gardens in T'ang China, raises the possibility that the prototype originally came from the continent.

K47 *Take bus 28 from the station to Daikakuji. Osawa-no-ike lies east of the temple: its grounds can be entered directly from the access road.*

Tenryuji

Kamakura Period

· ·

Looking across the pond to the *horai* island and *karedaki*.

Ashikaga Takauji converted a palace built for retired emperor Gosaga (reigned 1242–1246) to a Zen temple in the Kamakura period to appease the spirit of Emperor Godaigo, who had lived there as a child and whom he had deposed. Muso Soseki, who had advised Takauji to take this action, became the first abbot. He opened the temple in 1339, remodelling the garden about the same time.

Tenryuji's beautiful pond lies at the foot of hillsides rising to Arashiyama, included in the design as the oldest existing example of borrowed scenery. Two related rock groups, among the finest in Japan, can be seen at the far side. A great tumble of rocks down the bank forms Ryumon-no-taki, the Dragon Gate Waterfall, associated with the legend that says 'if a carp can climb the fall, it will turn into a dragon and enter heaven' (the carp is half-way up). Another group with an emphatic vertical thrust, rising above the water just right of a bridge, represents a *horai* island. Separately compelling, these groups together form a balanced and dynamic composition recalling the towering mountain scenes of Sung dynasty ink paintings.

K48 *Tenryuji is in the Arashiyama district, a popular destination in cherry-blossom time. Take the JR San-in line to Saga station or the Keifuku Dentetsu to Arashiyama station.*

Saihoji (Kokedera – Moss Temple)

Kamakura Period

Previously the paradise garden of a Jodo (Pure Land) Sect temple, Saihoji became a Zen temple in 1339 when Muso Soseki was appointed abbot.

The lower pond garden is bathed in an emerald glow reflected off rolling carpets of moss and gleaming sweeps of water. Tall, lichen-stippled trunks rise to a light-filtering canopy, small maples gracefully veil or channel understorey views. The visitors' path wanders past a small pond featuring a row of 'night mooring stones', around the main pond with its several bridge-connected islands, to a gate marking transition to the upper garden. Further on, left of the path, is a *kamejima* rock group. A small temple containing a statue of Soseki, sits at a high level below a three-tiered spill of rocks thought by most experts to be a dry waterfall. These rock compositions, usually attributed to Soseki, are among the earliest examples of their kind in Japan, inspiring many later gardens.

K49 *A Saihoji visit requires reservation well ahead of time (7–10 days) via self-addressed, return-postage paid postcards, and is expensive, but well worth the cost and effort. Postcards are available at the Tourist Information Centre or any post office. Take the Kyoto bus 73 from the station and get off at Kokedera.*

An old earth-covered bridge melds into the natural earth.

Katsura Imperial Villa

Edo Period

. . . .

Prince Toshihito (1579–1629), brother to Emperor Goyozei (reigned 1586–1611), commenced the creation of this masterpiece of architecture and garden design in 1615. His son Toshitada (1619–1662) added to the villa and improved the garden, so that by 1645 Katsura appeared much as it does today.

Design and details reflect the 'Enshu' style, although Kobori himself, long held to be the designer, may have had no direct involvement. Katsura results from a splendid fusion of his influence, the creativity of Princes Toshihito and Toshitada, and the skills of the artisans who carried out the work.

Katsura villa exemplifies the *sukiya* or 'buildings of refined taste' style. *Sukiya* style evolved from the more formal *shoin* style under the influence of tea ceremony architecture, whose origins were found in simple rural dwellings. It unites structural directness and free planning with sophisticated detailing. At Katsura an incremental procession of pavilions steps diagonally across the face of an elegant and meticulously maintained garden.

The garden, the earliest stroll garden, is formed around a pond whose convoluted form provides a maximum perimeter for its area. It is almost impossibly rich in stunning vistas, superb details, allusions to famous scenes from nature or literature, exquisitely composed stepping stones, bridges, lanterns and tea houses. Much may be familiar, for Katsura must be the most photographed and published garden in Japan, if not anywhere.

The Shokintei, or Pine and Harp Pavilion, graces Katsura's pond.

K50 *We are tempted to say 'stick with the photographs' as the conducted hour-long free tour permits only the scantiest overview. Book at the office of the Imperial Household Agency (see K4 Shugakuin). Katsura is on Hachijo-dori. Bus 33 runs from Kyoto station but is infrequent.*

KISSATEN:
AT HOME WITH COFFEE

喫茶店 Coffee shop. *Kissaten*. Its English sound implies romance – fortuitous hints of kisses and gentle sips, a slow seduction in coffee house peace. Already a fragrant spiral sucks you away. In written Japanese visual and phonetic layers slide beneath the verbal, with a marvellous capacity for additive meaning as simpler *kanji* group together to form more complex characters.

Henshall, in his *Guide to Remembering Japanese Characters*, traces this evolutionary process. The ideogram for 'mouth' 口 combines with a phonetic use of 契, 'join' or 'pledge' from an old meaning of making a pledge by matching notched tallies, to give kitsu 喫: 'chew in the mouth'. This became just 'take in/ingest through the mouth' (the intimacy of the mouth extends even to the slight frisson of teeth). The character *kitsu* compounds with sa 茶 'tea' and *ten* 店 'shop'. *Kissaten*: shop-where-you-take-in-tea-through-the-mouth. But in fact it's coffee. Takahashi Yasuo in *The Electric Geisha* points out that 'let's have a cup of tea' in Japan is actually an invitation to go to a coffee house. The sub-text that belies westernisation.

You may wonder why a discussion of coffee suddenly appears in a book on gardens, particularly as tea seems their proper accompaniment. An addictive part of our garden experience now is relaxing over coffee afterwards, as it has usually been either too expensive or uncomfortable to kneel sipping tea in the perfect spot. After all, it's quite appropriate, the *kissaten* being a natural descendant of the tea house. In the Meiji race to westernisation, the European coffee house was a natural import to a country where tea as a ritual for the tranquil meeting of minds had already

established a custom of meditative imbibing. Takahashi outlined the early rise in Meiji Tokyo of cafés in the French literary mode. The first was near Ueno in 1888, followed in the 1910s by Maison Kônosu, a writers' den serving strong French coffee, and Café Printemps, a salon for artists and writers started by painter Matsuyama Shozo. About the same time, 'milk halls', that sold coffee inexpensively in beer mugs, popularised the basic drink aside from aesthetic associations. By the 1930s *kissaten* were everywhere, including special coffee shops where for two or three times the standard cup price, a young man might discreetly converse with a young woman, to the strains of classical music.

Japanese coffee shop! Lacquer-bright syllables, lip-gloss reveries in a phrase inflected with metropolitan sleekness . . . Extravagant moments shimmer in memory: delicate porcelain, a flawless carnation in a fluted white vase, high-style chairs at Shibuya's elegant Bunkamura centre, green marble skirtings at Hiroshima Art Museum . . . or the airy elegance of Kyoto's Museum of Modern Art, designed by Maki Fumihiko, where his reinterpretation of the raised tea house frames summer greenery. From techno-glitz to snuggeries for Office Flowers, girls whose office duties are mainly workplace decoration – and all with the same top coffee as the Hikosan local, remote in Kyushu mountains. ('Blue Mountain' coffee there? Quite possibly.)

But that's megalopolis: mere glimpses of a world where coffee might cost $10 a cup, without ascending to the stratosphere of fabled coffee shops where the valuable cup becomes your own after consumption of its gold-dusted contents. (There's one in Nara apparently.) In big cities specialist *kissaten* mirror your every whim: there's a coffee shop just for you, playing your music, with your magazines, your style – a mirror for glamorous self perceptions. However on casual forays to smaller cities as a tourist umbilically tied to JR, you wallow in the last gasp of the Japanese coffee shop heyday, a traditional world fast disappearing. Every town has its little haven, warm and woodsy, like the one in Uwajima, where jazz pulses quietly among the gleaming timbers of naturally hewn tables and dark panelling, while the discreet proprietor waves his wand over glass coffee-makers and everything seems bathed in a golden-brown glaze. (Next day he bows to us from his bicycle.)

Post-war *kissaten*, along with *pachinko* parlours and love hotels, were invaluable as a rendezvous away from cramped housing and the formal pressures of Japanese society. The clandestine cocoon of a booth provided all home comforts – for breakfast, deals, dates, and for a young man, a place of refuge from examination hell and matriarchal claustrophobia. Thousands of *kissaten* were built prior to the inevitable shift of fashion that eventually resulted from the relaxation of import restrictions in 1960, causing coffee to become more of a home drink rather than an indispensable social focus. Nowadays fashion statements

are channelled more to establishments appealing to newer generations, to large chain-style restaurants, or international imports. Mr Donuts pops up dispiritingly here and there, while the original *kissaten* is declining in a timewarp, in railway station limbo-land and quiet suburban corners.

Furukawa: western dining under bright pink neon. Vast steins of excellent beer, plastic mats with picture menus, large cut-outs of kitchen equipment (spoons, toasters, stoves) as decoration on yellow walls – and a strange meal of lettuce and chicken upper arms, devoid of the flying bit. (The tired were desperate.)

Provincial (it's definitely a style, imprinted with European aspirations, with Meiji ghosts absorbing Paris) coffee shops seem to have been all built at once. At a certain moment the post-war coffee shop arrived – and stayed, stranded in a sixties trance, in an environment otherwise dizzy with renewal. Anywhere else these beautifully maintained period pieces would be several looks later, but in the true *kissaten*, sentimental trivia rules and orange is still this season's colour. Ironically they are the product of a time when kitsch achieved a popularity of critical derision, as popular culture became a shooting gallery for the commandos of the International Style. If seeking coffee *per se*, you enter a cycle of subtle entrapment. It's always the same. Insidious signifiers creep up on you and suddenly, there you are *again*, cradled in mission brown and Spanish stucco, burgundy plush and rococo vinyl, beside a sleepy china Mexican with his sombrero of tooth picks, and Buddha as guardian of the eternal verities. In this universal decor, the nicotine-encrusted air-conditioner lurks dimly under timber coffering and brass wall lights battle the comforting gloom. The sort of place where they play 'Smoke gets in your Eyes' and mean it.

Toe-to-toe at a tight-fit table for two, you sink into the ambience of a just-post-Elvis dreamtime. Dark timber and orange tiles waver in the aromatic haze as you yield to this fragrant embrace, reaching for your hot towel and glass of water, feebly muttering, 'Sumimasen, kohi . . . kohi o kudasai . . .' To which Mama-san's soothing response, immune to tentative Nihongo is a firm, 'Hotto?' Fussed over, you subside, subtly blandished into amae *– a state of dependence, childish yearning towards another for an unconditional love, where intimacy allows presumption. A great clue to the Japanese character, it has everything to do with desire, gut cries from the subconscious, a wish for inclusion.*

Wafting, dreamily anticipating, you watch the preparation. Having cornered the market for the world's best coffee beans, the Japanese lavish a minute attention on its preparation and serving that is an echo of the tea ceremony in its slow induction of relaxation and peace. Japan missed out on the Italian deluge that cascaded from Gaggia's 1946 espresso machine and flooded Australia. The influence remained more northerly – *Petit Tsuruoka, Restaurant and Cafe Bar Monsieur, Soirée, Cafe Mozart, Fellini's . . . Fellini's?* Ah . . . but the coffee isn't espresso in that *Dolce Vita* dive in Kumamoto. Just as *kissaten* flowered in the 1920s and 30s, so did vacuum coffee making, a process esteemed by Phillip Marlowe in *The Long Goodbye.* In most places the process is long considered 'outmoded because of the time and fidgeting

involved, and the unmatched breakability of the apparatus', as N. Kolpas says in *Coffee,* praising its 'classic elegance that cannot be matched by more modern automatic devices'. A natural for Japanese precise and ritualistic presentation, it's generally still made like this everywhere.

In the essential establishment, everyone sits along the counter behind their own apparatus. Coffee is placed in the upper part of the double glass coffee maker, with its previously fitted filter, and water in the bottom one; the two parts are screwed together at the waist. The whole is suspended over a gas burner. As the bottom flask heats, vapour expansion forces the water up through a central glass cylinder to the coffee above. After delicate stirring, at the exact moment, the contrivance is removed from the flame; the base cools, creating a vacuum below that sucks the filtered coffee back again, ready for your personal pour. It's great. There's never a Bad Coffee day in Japan.

Travel itself is a suspension of reality, of responsibility: the coffee shop is the suspension of travelling and all its divine discomfort – an amniotic hiatus. Such a reward after dancing your shoes into holes. The procedures certainly seem to smack of sorcery – the good witch's incantations, transformation at a mystic moment, the bubbling potion, the fairy wand, pixie-sized cream jugs – mythic properties; all without the bad bit of the fable. The Holy Grail in flowered Mikasa.

A travel diary word count: 'garden/s' (ostensibly the travel object), 87 times; 'train', 73 times: 'coffee', 35 times. At an average 350¥, a cup a day for a month can consume A$150 when the exchange rate is bad. Best not to examine such profligacy. Especially when lunch is otherwise a solitary banana from Ecuador, with which you feel a sudden third-world kinship.

'My Blue Heaven' murmurs, but it's not, it's my orange squishy vinyl heaven. Straw cushions de-sag old seats; crusty yellow-painted niches display cherished trinkets: driftwood, a china pig, fat scrotal badgers, bonsai, a gold dolphin, mini straw snowboots, kokeshi: little dolls, big dolls. Newspapers hang beside you – no need to stretch a lethargic hand. Ghettoblaster above the brick framed fridge. Flowered wallpaper behind glassware shelves tones with the ceiling's smoke-stained ochre. Beige lace door drapes, posters: Miyajima, Marie Laurencin, Chaplin, 'I love Kyoto' (I do, I do), Renoir . . . Impressionism is never far away in Japan. Hostess and friend idle away the morning, absorbed in TV talent time. We admire the baby. All relaxing together in daytime drowsiness . . .

GARDENS WEST AND SOUTH
OF KYOTO

Fumon-in

Koyasan • Wakayama Prefecture • Edo Period

. . . .

More than fifty *shukubo* (temple lodgings) cater for pilgrims and visitors in the historic monastic settlement of Koyasan, high in Wakayama's wild mountains. Many *shukubo* have attractive private gardens within their compounds, two of the more important being at Tentoku-in, where design is attributed to Kobori Enshu, and Fumon-in. The latter was probably built between 1688 and 1704, about the time the temple was established.

Fumon-in makes spectacular use of a steep, heavily wooded hillside enclosing the garden in a towering wall of foliage. In a narrow band of flat ground near the guest wings a small pond containing a turtle island meanders between stone-edged banks furnished with lanterns and bridges. Clipped bushes rise up the hillside to merge with maples, cryptomeria and other trees massed on the upper slopes. Among this foliage a large mounded hedge at the head of a dry cascade may symbolise distant mountains.

W1 *Fumon-in is near the central information office. A Koyasan visit should include a stay of one or two nights in temple lodgings so you can feel part of a garden as it changes mood through its daily cycle. And get away occasionally, from the day-trippers' cars that sometimes choke the narrow roads. Information offices in Koyasan supply maps of locations of various temple lodgings. (See map W1)*

Guests at Fumon-in look out over this splendid array of foliage from their bedroom windows.

Kongobuji

Koyasan • Wakayama Prefecture • Showa Period

• •

Kongobuji's dry garden.

Kongobuji, headquarters of the Koyasan Shingon Sect, was founded in 1593 by Toyotomi Hideyoshi as a memorial to his mother. The present building, an 1863 reconstruction, contains several Momoyama-period screens.

A spacious modern *karesansui* garden known as Banryutei wraps around a pavilion behind the main temple structure. Covering 2340 square metres (about 2800 square yards), Banryutei contains one hundred and forty granite rocks from Shikoku, some very large, set in white sand from the Kyoto area. The entire composition is said to symbolise two dragons in a sea of clouds guarding Okuno-in, the mausoleum of Kobo Daishi, founder of Shingon Buddhism. Originally known as Kukai, he established Koyasan monastery in 817.

W2 *Kongobuji is in the main street in Koyasan.*

Momijidani Garden

Wakayama • Wakayama Prefecture • Edo Period

. . . .

Tokugawa Yorinobu, founder of the Kishu Tokugawa clan, built Momijidani Garden in the early Edo period for Nishinomaru Palace, which lay on level ground to the north.

The garden has two distinct parts: an open spread of water utilising the moat and walls of Wakayama Castle on the east, and a western area designed around a richly wooded hillside. Engyokaku, a small cypress-bark roofed pavilion set over water on granite piers, links the two sections, establishing a focal point for the entire garden. Streams and waterfalls

Engyokaku, a small pavilion at the edge of the ruined castle's moat.

tumble down through lush western hillside growth into a calm pond where a boat rock sails across green reflections, and boldly scaled Kishu bluestone rocks are lavishly disposed in the Momoyama style. Here and there are bridges in timber and stone construction, the ruins of a tea room and a parlour, and a recently built (air-conditioned) tea room. The garden would be at its best in May, when azaleas are in bloom, or late autumn for maple colour.

W3 *Momijidani Garden is about 15 minutes' walk from Wakayama-shi station.*

Kishiwada Castle

Kishiwada • Osaka Prefecture • Showa Period

Shigemori's dynamic garden dominated by its central 'generalissimo' rock.

Koide Hidemasa, a nephew of Toyotomi Hideyoshi, built a five-storey donjon at Kishiwada Castle late in the sixteenth century. Lightning destroyed it early in the nineteenth century, and the present three-storey concrete replacement was built in 1954 as a museum. Shigemori Mirei designed the forecourt garden.

The garden is called Hachijin-no-niwa, or Garden of Eight Battle Formations, referring to battle tactics said to have been employed by Zhu-Ge Liang, a warlord in ancient China. Rock groups representing the eight formations are distributed in a roughly circular arrangement around a central group where one rock, the supreme commander, towers above all others. The groups stand in white sand on three levels separated by angular stone walls, and the design overall is said to be based on the layout of the castle in the Muromachi period. Safety-mesh screens unfortunately interfere with views from the castle tower, the place where the garden's abstract qualities can be seen most completely.

W4 *Kishiwada Castle is about 15 minutes' walk from Kishiwada station, on the Nankai Main Line between Wakayama-shi and Namba (on the Osaka subway system). A map outside the station shows the way.*

Honpukuji (Mizumi-do)

Oiso, Awaji Island • Hyogo Prefecture • Heisei Period

. . . .

An austere approach belies the temple's sumptuous interior.

Honpukuji's 1991 main hall, the Mizumi-do (Water Temple), was built on a hillside with extensive views over Osaka Bay, to a design by Ando Tadao, one of Japan's most admired architects. Far from exploiting the site's obvious attributes, he has created a subterranean other-world roofed by an oval dish filled with water and planted with lilies and lotuses. A stairway shaft penetrates this artificial pond, leading down to the sanctuary, where the austere concrete shell houses an independent and visually sumptuous framework of red-painted timber posts, screens and lattices, containing the altar.

The temple is approached across a rising plane of white gravel along a twisting entry path that leads to a small opening in a free-standing concrete wall. The path turns to hug a second curved wall that ends in a sharp left turn to reveal the pond along an axis diagonal to the stairway. These simple elements, plus the animating reflections of trees and sky, are assembled into an intriguing garden that denies its overt minimalism through allusions to traditional features such as lotus ponds, and the entry passageway manipulations of Shisendo or Jiko-in.

The lotus pond.

W5 *Oiso is reached from the mainland by buses travelling across the new Akashi Kaikyo Bridge from the stop above the Maiko station on the JR San'yo Main Line. From the Oiso bus stop walk south down the main road then turn west by the* koban, *uphill to the temple.*

Kozenji

Tottori • Tottori Prefecture • Edo Period

. . . .

Kozenji's garden in early summer.

The Ikeda family temple, Ryuhoji, was moved from Okayama to Tottori in 1632. Its name was changed to Kozenji in 1693, when the garden had already been established.

The pond-viewing garden nestles against a luxuriantly wooded hillside north of the *shoin*. Rocks, scattered over the mound behind the pond and mingled with bushes, consolidate to the west in a *karedaki*, with a fine *kamedejima* at its foot. A vine-clad earth bridge crosses the pond towards the east. Although bushes tend to overpower the mound's rock arrangements, Kozenji's overall composition is simple and finely balanced, effectively dramatised by the tonal density of its background foliage.

W6 *Kozenji is easily reached via buses up the main road running north-east from the station. Maps are available at the station tourist information office. Kannon-in, a better-known garden, is about 1 kilometre (²/₃ mile) further south along the foothills.*

Korakuen

Okayama • Okayama Prefecture • Edo Period

. . . .

Ikeda Tsunamasa, a daimyo of the Bizen fief, commenced building the garden now called Korakuen in 1687. The Ikeda family retained possession until 1884, when it became a public park. Dating from 1871, the name Korakuen (The Garden for Taking Pleasure Later) refers to an old Chinese saying 'the lord must bear sorrow before the people, take pleasure after them'.

Sleek lawns in late afternoon sun at Korakuen.

Korakuen occupies a 13.3-hectare (32.9-acre) site on the north bank of the Asahi river opposite the black, rather menacing face of Okayama castle, which appears in many views as borrowed scenery. Spacious lawns surround a central large pond, Sawa-no-ike (Marshy Pond), containing three islands and said to represent the scenery of Lake Biwa. Arranged around this open centre are groves of maple, plum, cherry and pine trees, a tea plantation, a rice field laid out in the old Chinese style of 3 x 3 squares, a woodland with a waterfall and other scenic and seasonal delights. Streams wind between ponds, one flowing through the centre of an elegant, airy pavilion called Ryuten (Tea Shop by the Stream) where poetry parties were held. A zig-zag timber bridge (*yatsuhashi*) crosses an iris bed nearby. The only artificial mountain, Yuishinsan (Sole Heart Mountain), rises above clusters of immaculate azalea hedges to offer panoramic views from its summit.

W7 *Korakuen lives up to its lofty reputation. From the station take either the Higashiyama tram to Shiroshita stop, or Okaden bus from stand 9 to Korakuen-mae stop. Good English language pamphlets issued on entrance. Free if you're over 65.*

Tokoen

Okayama • Okayama Prefecture • Edo Period

A peaceful pond to stroll around, where boats lie under trees and irises edge the banks.

Ikeda Tadakatsu, a daimyo of the Bizen fief, constructed this garden for relaxation in the seventeenth century, some seventy years before Korakuen. He named it Tokugetsudai (Moon Gaining Place). The garden, said to have retained its original structure and being carefully maintained by its present owners, offers a peaceful alternative to Korakuen.

Tokoen is roughly square in shape and measures about 3300 square metres (0.8 acres) in area. Most of the space is taken up with a central pond designed for boating enjoyment as well as perimeter strolls. The pond's longer axis runs diagonally across the site from north-east to south-west, while a counterpointing diagonal axis links a villa on the pond's edge with the garden's principal focal point, a tall stone pagoda on a mound in the south-east corner of the site. The garden's composition originally included a view of distant Higashiyama, now lost to urban development.

W8 *Take the Higashiyama tram from Okayama station; get off at Kadotayashiki stop (third after Kyobashi Bridge). Tokoen is entered off a side street running south from the stop.*

Achi Shrine

Kurashiki • Okayama Prefecture • Probably prehistoric

. . . .

Several ancient rock groups at the Achi Shrine, on the summit of Tsurugatayama in central Kurashiki, were venerated before the Shrine was built, probably in the Muromachi period. They are bound with *shimenawa*, indicating a sacred presence.

A group with crane and turtle island components west of the main shrine may also signify Mt Horai. In the rear north-west corner, a neglected *karedaki* tumbles down through bushes away from the summit, overhung lower down by a huge, trellis-supported wisteria said to be over five hundred years old, best viewed from the path

Shimenawa bind these sacred rocks; offered to their *kami* is a modern drink.

below. Further groups to the north-east include a beautifully weathered *iwakura* (a rock worshipped for the presence of a deity).

W9 *Tsurugatayama Park adjoins the historical section of the city. It is an easy walk (about 20 minutes) from the station following maps available in the information office.*

Raikyuji

Takahashi • Okayama Prefecture • Edo Period

· ·

Raikyuji's unparalleled combination of sculptured hedges and rock groupings.

Kobori Enshu governed Matsuyama district for 15 years following the death of his father, the previous governor, in 1604. He lived at Raikyuji during this time, and is generally presumed to have designed the garden that lies in front of the *shoin*. It has one of the most spectacular examples of *o-karikomi* in Japan.

A large azalea hedge, shaped like tumbling ocean waves, runs along one side of the garden in front of a tall, enclosing bank of camellias. Lower hedges on the far side allow distant Mt Atago to appear as borrowed scenery. The garden's principal focus, an island of rocks and low intertwining hedges, lies across a sea of white, raked sand. This composition includes a striking triad, and is usually interpreted as a crane island, or possibly Shumisen. A curving row of stepping stones across the sand recalls Enshu's garden at Konchi-in, Kyoto; paving stones and pebbles under eaves are later additions.

W10 *Bitchu-Takahashi is 40 minutes from Kurashiki on the Hakubi Line. Raikyuji is about 15 minutes' walk north of the station, where a map is displayed. Walk down the main road in front of the station to a stream. Cross and turn right, then left after crossing a railway line. The temple is a short distance along on the right.*

Ritsurin Park

Takamatsu • Kagawa Prefecture • Edo Period

Ritsurin Park has one of the finest large daimyo stroll gardens. Sanuki fuedal lord Ikoma Takatoshi established a residence with a pond garden here during the Momoyama period, at the base of Shiunsan (Purple Cloud Mountain). Matsudaira daimyos owned the property during the Edo period, enlarging the garden over a span of several generations until its completion in 1745.

The most interesting section of the present park is the older south garden, where the tea house known as Kikugetsutei (Moon Scooping Pavilion), originally constructed c 1640, overlaps the edge of South Pond, and superb views include the wooded slopes and the profile of Shiunsan as borrowed scenery. Trees are trimmed shapes like flattened hat boxes, and bushes clipped in cubic forms show 'box-making' or *hako-zukuri* topiary.

W11 *The easiest way to Ritsurin from Takamatsu JR station is via the Kotoden bus; get off at Kotoden Ritsurin-mae stop, a minute's walk from the garden.*

The old south garden under snow; an unexpected happening in warmer Shikoku.

Chikurin-in

Tokushima • Tokushima Prefecture • Edo Period

Lush flowers in summer rain.

In 1674 the Obaku Zen Sect founded Chikurin-in on the site of an earlier Shingon Sect temple destroyed in civil war.

The garden, dating from 1684, is now attractively overgrown. A long, relatively narrow pond lies in the space between the *shoin* and a hillside. A barely visible dry waterfall rises from the right-hand end while away to the left the pond almost disappears behind bushes and islands. A thirteen-storey stone pagoda on the hillside across the pond provides the major focal point; a number of weathered lanterns offer subsidiary points of interest. Stepping stones and bridges are made with bluestone from nearby sources that splits into thin, strong and beautifully textured slabs.

W12 *On our rain-drenched visit, clouds hung low, only drifting occasionally to disclose mountain-top* shakkei. *The* koban *near the station rang ahead to ensure the garden was open. Take a bus from the station to Chikurin-in-mae and walk up the hill. (See map W12)*

Senshukaku Teien

Tokushima • Tokushima Prefecture • Momoyama Period

. . . .

Tokushima castle no longer exists, but a garden built about 1590 and once attached to a *shoin* in the grounds remains preserved at Tokushima-chuo-koen, a park a few minutes' walk from Tokushima station. The name Senshukaku (Pavilion of a Thousand Autumns) dates from 1908.

Senshukaku Teien uses massive, strikingly textured blue-grey rocks in flamboyant profusion as banks, bridges, stepping stones, Mt Horai and other groups in and around a pond and mountain garden, and a

A 'dry' garden in teeming rain, after visiting Chikurin-in.

nearby *karesansui* garden. A stone bridge, approximately 10 metres (34 feet) long, linking crane and turtle islands in the *karesansui* garden, is probably the longest in Japan. Pines, cherry trees, azalea bushes and cycads among other plants decorate hills and banks. Although sitting rather incongruously among manicured lawns, Senshukaku Teien displays the arrogance and bravura that characterised Momoyama castle architecture and gardens.

W13 *Senshukaku Teien is located at the eastern end of Tokushima-chuo-koen, which lies between railway tracks and a river north-east of Tokushima station. Walk east along the road in front of the station, then north across the tracks to the park. (See map W12)*

Hokokuji

Saijo • Ehime Prefecture • Muromachi Period

. . . .

Shadows hide Hokokuji's complex two-step dry waterfall.

The provenance of Hokokuji's pond garden, a survivor of wars and temple reconstructions, has been rather loosely ascribed to Soami. While this may be questionable, it does possess some of the most sophisticated and evocative rock groupings seen outside Kyoto.

Views from the temple focus on an 'ink-painting' scene under trees in the left-hand corner, where craggy mountains tower above a double-tiered waterfall. The waterfall, formed with a pair of flat-topped rocks, descends to the pond where a large turtle island lies just off-shore. Islets, a bridge, several triads, and a *horai* rock to the south with a small *karedaki* to its right complete a rich sequence of rock groups.

W14 *The temple lies in foothills overlooking pleasant countryside and is set behind an attractive forecourt with a pond, cycads, stepping stones through moss and the remains of an overgrown moat. It is easily reached by taxi in a little under 10 minutes from the station – there are infrequent buses along a highway not far away.*

Fukada Residence

Yonago • **Tottori Prefecture** • **Kamakura Period**

Legend ascribes this garden's construction to a time when Emperor Godaigo (reigned 1318–1339) stayed at the old family residence. It surrounds a pond with crane and turtle islands and features a *karedaki* topped by three towering rocks in the right-hand corner. A space filled with gravel and moss beds, clipped bushes and stepping stones separates the pond from a shelter where visitors are served tea as they enjoy the garden; remaining sides are walled in. The small garden is beautifully kept, and while the *karedaki/sanzon* group looks uncomposed, as if reconstructed, the two islands are wonderfully realised in fissured, eroded rocks that suggest long exposure to wild elements.

In this cosily scaled garden, a turtle island is opposed by a fierce crane head.

W15 *Like many gardens off the beaten track, the Fukada Residence offers an hour or two of quiet pleasure and is well worth a stop-over in Yonago. It is 10 minutes from the station by taxi, 15 by bus, or 10 minutes' walk east of the Higashiyama Park station (one stop east of Yonago). The residence is on the south side of the first road north of the railway line, about 4 minutes' walk west of a river. (See map W15)*

Adachi Museum Gardens

Sagi-no-onsen • Shimane Prefecture • Showa Period

. . . .

A *tour de force* of meticulous maintenance, these gardens in the traditional manner, elegantly designed by Nakane Kinsaku, cover about 43,000 square metres (10.6 acres) of land around the Adachi Museum, which shows early modern Japanese paintings and ceramics. Collection and gardens celebrate joint passions of the museum's founder, the late Adachi Zenko, who is quoted saying, 'The garden is, so to speak, a picture scroll.'

Gardens do indeed unroll before your gaze as you virtually experience a stroll garden without leaving the building. Its wings, courts, corridors and windows are arranged to give a sequence of direct, diagonal and framed views of the four principal gardens. You first encounter the Dry Landscape Garden, a multi-layered composition extending from a gravel foreground through intermediate zones of undulating grass, clipped bushes, miniaturised trees and rocks, then backing groves of trees, to distant hills. Diverting around the Moss Garden, you return to the first garden which flows into the White Gravel and Pine Garden, from whose foreground pond an extraordinary vista rises over white gravel slopes studded with miniaturised trees to the *shakkei* of a 15-metre (50-feet) high waterfall falling down a rock face on the other side of the main road outside. The fourth garden is the relatively intimate Pond Garden.

The gardens include spectacular examples of exaggerated perspective and *shakkei*, the former confusing normal perceptions of scale, the latter vastly extending their limits.

The White Gravel and Pine Garden, its waterfall beyond.

W16 *Buses run from Yasugi station on the San-in Main Line; the trip takes about 30 minutes. Foreign visitors with their passports enter the museum at a concession rate.*

Kokokuji

Hirata • Shimane Prefecture • Edo Period

. . . .

Kokokuji is thought to date from the Kamakura period. The gentle present-day garden was completed in 1837. A *karesansui* garden overlooks a reservoir at the foot of Mt Tabushi's wooded slopes. These three elements form the basic structure of a composition which is quietly elaborated with stepping stones and rustic paths across the gravel plane, a tall lantern and, on the right-hand side, a screen of trimmed hedges and bamboo fences. The garden's design is credited to Sawa Gentan, a prominent gardener previously employed by Matsudaira Fumai (1751–1818), seventh lord of Matsue.

W17 *Just as visiting Kokokuji is a relaxed experience in tranquil and beautiful surroundings, the journey there from Matsue on the private Ichibata Electric Railway is one of those small-train trips that can make travel in rural Japan such a joy. Sometimes it runs along the edge of Lake Shinji, sometimes through leafy channels, and sometimes between ricefields where isolated farmhouses stand behind windbreaks of trimmed pine trees like great lacy lattices. Leave the train at Tabushi station (one beyond Hirata-shi); after crossing route 431, walk north-west for about 10 minutes up the road at right angles to the railway line. Kokokuji is off to the left. (See map W17)*

A most peaceful and welcoming place, with its dry garden above a steep bank down the lake.

Shukkeien

Hiroshima • Hiroshima Prefecture • Edo Period

Daimyo Asano Nagakira began building Shukkeien in 1620, the year after he took up residence in Hiroshima castle. Ueda Soko, his principal retainer and a tea master, oversaw construction. A landscape gardener from Kyoto named Shimizu Shichiroemon carried out improvements between 1783 and 1788 on behalf of Asano Shigeakira. Presented to Hiroshima Prefecture in 1940, Shukkeien was fire-gutted by the atomic bomb explosion of 1945. Post-war restoration work has matured to recapture the garden's former grace, and Shukkeien now offers visitors to this emblematic city a life-enhancing alternative to the Peace Memorial Park's sombre theme.

Shukkeien, literally 'shrink-scenery garden', is a typical Edo period stroll garden built around a central pond dotted with islands and islets and bisected by Kokokyo (Straddling Rainbow Bridge) a bold stone structure dating from the time of the 1783–88 improvements. Paths around the pond encounter artificial mountains and valleys, orchards, special display plantings such as hydrangeas and irises, arbours and a *sukiya*-style shingle-roofed pavilion among other features. The total area is about 4 hectares (10 acres).

The original bridge, survivor of atomic devastation.

W18 *The garden is about 12 minutes' walk west of JR Hiroshima station on the south side of Kyobashi River. The station's information office has maps.*

Tsuki no Katsura Garden

Hofu • Yamaguchi Prefecture • Edo Period

. . . .

Katsura Tadaharu, principal councillor to Mori Migita, a Mori clan leader, built this little L-shaped rock and sand garden alongside his residence in 1712.

The hare rock, focus of a lunar celebration every 23 November.

According to an interpretation offered by the residence, the eastern part depicts an ancient Chinese Buddhist tale of a hare and an oyster that became pregnant by absorbing moonlight: an allegorical expression of the enlightenment that can be achieved when human intelligence is as pure and innocent as conception by means of the light of the moon. The hare is represented by a striking switch-back rock mounted on a rock pedestal and the oyster by a nearby round flat rock. The longer, south side of the garden is said to portray a realm of the immortals.

In another interpretation, the switch-back rock is a boat rock, while we wonder if there is a local landscape reference to a startlingly similar rock on a nearby hill-top, seen from the *shinkansen*. Such ambiguities, intriguing as they are, may remain unresolved: the garden stands on the merits of its abstract presence alone.

W19 *Buses to Tsuki no Katsura leave from Hofu station at varying intervals; timetables and maps are available from the Tourist Information Centre located in the station building. The trip takes 11 minutes. Get off at the first stop after passing under the railway, walk back a bit and turn towards the hills. You see the walled garden across a small vegetable patch. (See map W19)*

W20 Mori Residence

Hofu • Yamaguchi Prefecture • Meiji Period

. . . .

The spacious pond below the Mori Residence.

Mori Motonori built this villa and garden after surrendering to Emperor Meiji the Choshu fiefdom which the Mori family had ruled from Hagi during the Edo period. The large garden is designated as a Cultural Asset by the Yamaguchi Prefecture, and the villa, now a museum, is noted for exhibiting a famous Sesshu painting.

The villa overlooks a garden built on various levels above a broad pond with high steep banks, branching on the near side into a narrow inlet at the foot of a rocky ravine. Views across the pond highlight a decorative stone bridge crossing the inlet, and also take in nearby hills as borrowed scenery. Rock groupings and other details, notably a gigantic stone snow-viewing lantern, are executed in a massive scale, as if to be viewed from within the villa rather than close by.

W20 *The Mori Residence is about 30 minutes' walk from the station. Closed Sundays. (See map W19)*

Joeiji

Yamaguchi • Yamaguchi Prefecture • Muromachi Period

. . . .

Sesshu lived in Yamaguchi from about 1484 until the turn of the century. He is believed to have built a garden at Myokiji, a temple constructed in 1455, now called Joeiji.

Hillside trees embrace a garden built around a pond and separated from the main building by a spread of softly undulating grass. Across this small rocks are arranged individually or in small groups, sometimes triads. Supplemented by low, clipped bushes, they are said to symbolise mountains in China or Mt Fuji. The pond is divided into two parts by opposing

Flat topped rocks reminiscent of Sesshu's paintings.

peninsulas linked by an earth-covered bridge. The part nearer the building contains turtle and crane islands and a splendid boat rock, the rear section a rock islet. A rugged waterfall composition descends a little gully in the north-east. Sesshu built up forms in his paintings with short, angularly related, straight lines. He echoed this vocabulary here through the selection of flat-topped, straight-sided rocks: scenes of mountains, ravines, islands and seas are realised as three-dimensional versions of his own paintings.

W21 *Joeiji is about 3 kilometres (2 miles) north-east of Yamaguchi station and about 8 minutes by taxi. Buses run along route 9 from the downtown area and the station; get off half a kilometre (about 500 yards) before the route 262 flyover and walk north towards the hills. Joeiji is about 12 minutes' walk away.*

GARDENS AT MASUDA, SHIMANE PREFECTURE

W22 and W23

. . . .

The artist Sesshu visited Masuda when he was living at Yamaguchi during the last sixteen years of the fifteenth century, and gardens at two temples are sometimes attributed to him.

Ikoji

Edo Period

. . . .

Ikoji was built in the sixteenth century on the grounds of a burned-down older temple. The fact that Sesshu is known to have visited is no doubt the source of the debatable story of his having built the existing garden. The temple itself seems convinced, however, proudly naming it the Sesshu Garden. Ikoji was itself destroyed and rebuilt on two occasions, first in the mid-seventeenth century when the garden was probably constructed, and again in the eighteenth century.

Ikoji seems set in some dense forest, the sky barely visible from its verandah overlooking a small pond. A steep hillside rises through tiers of clipped, flat-topped azalea bushes and hedges to a crown of massed trees, a repetition of horizontal and vertical planes leading the eye away into deep forest shadows. At the same time, these geometric shapes tie the background to the temple's structure, creating a spacious feeling in an intimate enclosure. Behind the pond, to the left, is a dry waterfall, while on the right a large cherry tree overhangs the pond. A turtle island directs its head towards the waterfall and supports a *horai* rock showing the crisply defined surfaces preferred by Sesshu. Among other noteworthy rock compositions, a promontory near the foot of the waterfall suggests a crane peninsula. An islet quite graphically resembles a swimming turtle.

W22 *Ikoji is about 30 minutes' walk east of the JR station. Or catch a bus in the main street to Orito bus stop and cross the river. Maps are available in the* koban: *walk from the station to the main street, turn right; the* koban *is set back from the road a short distance along. (See map W22)*

Tiers of sharp fresh greenery ascend from pond to leafy hilltops at Ikoji.

Mampukuji

Muromachi Period

. . . .

Rocks in Mampukuji's striking Shumisen composition have the strong angular forms that characterise Sesshu's paintings and his garden at Joeiji, and the whole feeling of this garden seems much more in accord with his design style than does that of Ikoji. The central peak, rising above outer ranges on a gentle grass-covered mound and silhouetted against background foliage, provides the garden's focal point. A long narrow-waisted pond edged by small, relatively fussy rocks occupies the centre-ground, and the grassy foreground includes a large meditation stone. There is a tree-sheltered dry waterfall on the right-hand side where the pond widens to include a peninsula. Clipped bushes are few, allowing uncluttered expression of rock compositions.

W23

Mampukuji is about 10 minutes' walk from Ikoji. (See map W22)

Shumisen and *karedaki* compositions at Mampukuji.

Kyu Kameishi-bo

Near Hikosan • Fukuoka Prefecture • Muromachi Period

. . . .

Sesshu built the garden of Kyu Kameishi-bo while living at Hikosan after returning from China in 1469. Saved by remoteness from pillaging and alteration, it is probably the most intact if least tended of his surviving gardens.

The garden lies amid the magnificent forests, ranges and valleys of the Yaba-Hita-Hikosan Quasi National Park. At first it seems like a tumble of rocks in some roughly cleared ground on the edge of a hamlet, but looking closer you see a pond shaped like a sharply winding stream with fine rock groupings and areas sufficiently maintained to be distinguished from surrounding woodland. A waterfall composition rises above one bend,

A waterfall rock group in rustic surroundings.

while a tall conical rock symbolising Horai stands in the water near another. Some clipped azalea bushes around the pond belie the sense of nature barely kept at bay: wild plants grow among the rocks, while the understorey to the enclosing forest is rough and natural looking. In all, the atmosphere is rustic and, in the presence of such a timeless monument, reverential.

W24 *The JR train takes about 90 minutes from Kokura to Hikosan. A local bus from the station winds through forests for about 20 minutes to Bessho, a car-park lookout with a coffee shop. Kyu Kameishi-bo is a few minutes' walk on the left along the road uphill past the coffee shop.*

Komyoji

Dazaifu • Fukuoka Prefecture • Showa Period

. . . .

Komyoji, founded in 1273, belongs to the Tofukuji School of Rinzai Zen Buddhism. It has two modern gardens designed by Shigemori Mirei, who also designed gardens at the Tofukuji headquarters in Kyoto.

The main garden, the Ittekikai-tei (One-drop Ocean Garden) lies at the rear of the temple. Two right-angled wings of the temple and a bank running diagonally across the back of the garden enclose a triangular space furnished with curvy moss beds, raked white sand, weathered lichen-stippled rocks and young maple trees. Moss and sand beds combine in swirling forms representing land masses, islands and seas. Moss climbs the rear bank to merge with bamboos and mature trees; young maples meet overhead in a light-filtering canopy.

The Bukko Garden in front of the temple contains rocks in groups of 3–5–7, arranged to form the Chinese character for light.

W25 Komyoji is a few minutes' walk from Dazaifu station at the end of the Nishitetsu Dazaifu Line. Leave JR Kagoshima Main Line at Futsukaichi station, walk for about 10 minutes to Futsukaichi station on the Nishitetsu Omuta Line and take the Dazaifu train; another 10 minutes.

Green islands of moss in formalised curves
like clouds in ancient paintings.

Suizenji Park (Jojuen)

Kumamoto • Kumamoto Prefecture • Edo Period

• •

In 1632 daimyo Hosakawa Tadatoshi founded a temple named Suizenji on the site of the present garden. The temple was moved later, and a tea house was built on the vacated site, which was renamed Jojuen and further developed by later Hosokawa lords of Higo province. Jojuen became a public park in 1879.

A stroll garden in size and circulation, Jojuen is famous for one particularly striking image: a miniature version of Mt Fuji rising dramatically above undulating, grassy hills across the reflecting waters of a large pond. Perspective is exaggerated by progressively scaling down miniature trees. The closer they are to the summit the smaller they become. If the distraction of other normally scaled elements is mentally eliminated, vast distances are implied, an illusion even more apparent as you wander enclosed among the hills beyond.

Concerning distractions, a stall tucked in among those scenic hills destroys any sense of another world so painstakingly created by the gardeners. Jojuen must be the most commercialised garden in Japan. Food and souvenir shops dominate the space from which you view 'Mt Fuji' across the pond. Add the sales pitch of the professional photographer as he teases elderly tourists into tiers for the mandatory group photo, the hustle and bustle as groups arrive, rapidly circumnavigate and depart, the chattering waves of indifferent school children, and the atmosphere is far more festive than reflective. Yet Jojuen remains a fascinating garden, with exquisite details such as the *sawatobi-ishi*, or 'stepping stones across a marsh', a line of flat rocks stretching across the pond.

W26 *Jojuen looks splendid in summer when the grass is lush and green and surrounding trees conceal city buildings, but equally fine in winter when golden grass and low light emphasises the modelling of the mounds. Go early and avoid the crowds. Take the route 2 tram from the station, or tram routes 2 or 3 from downtown. Get off at Suizenji-koen-mae stop, walk north, then east.*

In a garden of 'famous view' allusions, Mt Fuji hovers as centrepiece, above the *sawatobi-ishi* rocks in the pond.

Chiran Samurai Residences

Chiran • Kagoshima Prefecture • Edo Period

. . . .

The small, hill-town of Chiran retains a street of houses built by samurai who accompanied their lord, head of the Shimazu clan, on his alternate year attendance in Edo. Gardeners from Kyoto, where the daimyo and his retinue dallied for cultural refreshment on their return trip, are said to have laid out their gardens.

Five gardens share a similar design. In each a plane of white sand sets a composition of rocks and clipped bushes apart from the house. The rocks build up to a towering climax, representing some mountainous crag given scale by a nearby stone pagoda. A tall closely-cropped hedge behind the rocks suggests a further range of mountains yet permits a view of actual distant mountains. A deep gully emerges from between the rocks as a river flowing into a sea. Decoratively trimmed pine trees flank and give subsidiary support to the rock formations.

Two gardens differ from this standard conception.

The Mori Residence estate, built in 1741 by a high ranking retainer at the foot of the old castle, contains the only pond garden in Chiran. In other ways, with its two-stepped hedge, sculptural rock forms and distinctive black pine, this garden resembles those previously described.

At the Mori Residence a curiously arched rock curves over the pond; tiny plants lodge in crevices.

· ·

At the Hirayama Residence, a large double-stepped hedge, modulated to frame distant mountain views, curves around the far side of the garden. Stone appears only in the form of pedestals aligned in front of the hedge, apparently as bases for displays. The austerity of this design seems to relate it intellectually closer to Kyoto than its stereotypical neighbours.

Distant hills define the valley's end beyond the Hirayama Residence.

W27 *Flanked by hedges with undulatory profiles tiered above stone walls, this street of houses and gardens is one of the most evocative microcosms of lost Japan. Buses leave from the Yamakataya bus terminal in Kagoshima town centre. There are ten trips daily, of which three stop at Nishi Kagoshima station en-route. The trip takes about 80 minutes. The admission price includes seven houses; there are a couple of entry points to the closed-off street.*

Iso Teien

Kagoshima • Kagoshima Prefecture • Edo Period

• •

Hazy Sakurajima, from Iso Teien's promenade.

The Shimazu clan dominated the Satsuma region for about seven hundred years from the Heian period until the Meiji Restoration, and in 1658 Mitsuhisa, the nineteenth lord, commenced building the villa and garden that is now one of Kagoshima's major attractions. The garden was extensively restored between 1830 and 1844. The winding stream Kyokusui Garden, believed to have been built in 1702 by the twenty-first lord, was restored after being rediscovered in 1959.

Iso Teien captures the profile and ash plumes of volcanic Sakurajima across the bay as borrowed scenery, a dramatic image now interrupted at lower levels by electricity standards. The garden, rising up a hillside above a broad and rather open base along the harbour front, is bisected by a large stone-lined ravine. A delicately landscaped pond adjoins the villa; groves of plum and bamboo and the Kyokusui Garden lie at higher levels. While Iso Teien, with its wide promenades, has more the atmosphere of a pleasure park than a great daimyo garden's intensity and richness, Sakurajima ominously dreaming makes a fascinating backdrop.

W28 *Iso Teien is about 10 minutes by Hayashida line bus 11 from Kagoshima station, or 35 minutes from Nishi Kagoshima station on route 10. The rather steep admission price includes entrance to Shoko Shuseikan built in 1865 and said to be Japan's first modern factory. It is now a museum of Shimazu relics.*

JOY OF THE
BUSINESS HOTEL

Ueno: A room too crowded when the television is on.

Chasing gardens on a railpass invites an intimate relationship with the railway station – its number of steps, the tempting plastic food displays of its eateries, the quality of its underground arcades for entertainment and quick shopping, 24-hour convenience stores, coffee shops, post-prandial sessions at the booking office – and the *bijinesu hoteru*, the ubiquitous business hotel. The needs of fast-moving foreigners dumped metaphorically blindfolded in a provincial city conveniently resemble those of the Japanese commuter – including quick departures. Most travel books speak of *ryokan* joys, of futons and fragrant meals brought by polite maids, of relaxing in cypress tubs viewing virgin forest, or communing in a rocky snow-girt hot spring; a magazine world unsuitable for a tight schedule and not within our budget.

We are more at home with the simple pleasures of the business hotel, beside or above the railway station, without having tackled the minimal ultimate of the capsule hotel, whose most architecturally famous example flanks an expressway in Tokyo's Shimbashi area. We have achieved intimacy with Takayama's railway yards, viewed the military quadrille of Fukui station's taxi formation and gazed sideways at Hikone castle in miniature between wall and affixed downpipe.

Kagoshima, southern Kyushu: obscure glass slides open – to rusty tin at arm's length. The room's slight grime is excused by the invisible smoke plume of volcano Sakurajima lazing across the bay. Brown drifts of ash lie on cars and morning television's wind diagram forecasts a non-washing day.

Unexpectedly, one of the cosy things about urban Japan for travellers is that everywhere is so much like everywhere else, a westernised homogeneity that is perhaps monotonous or ugly, but has a comfortable similarity: getting off the train at the other end of the country, you still feel at home. As you step into a new town you feel you left yesterday – aside from new wonders like a magnificent castle up the street – the business hotel is motel equivalent for the travelling salaryman, usually offering the spotless consistency of high comfort beds, unfailing hot water and a one-piece plastic bathroom module, with standing-room-only tub conveniently accessible to all facilities.

Furukawa, northern Honshu: If there's a steaming communal bath, beware of fainting from overlong immersion. Loss of consciousness is better achieved when out of the bath but still very alarming to your anxiously fanning partner.

It's possible to book business hotels from outside the country if you write: quaintly charming replies may induce over-expectation of a personal welcome. Perhaps actual *gaijin* presence is too discomforting, but essentially business hotels are not places for service. Reception personnel welcome the previously fictional guest with the warm detachment of public manners.

And yet . . . Okayama: Our charming host blinks with excitement, asking 'Why?' of our unprecedented stay of five nights – we're railpass commuting to Shikoku and Awaji Island. This basement entrance hoteru has the dull charm of cheapness two minutes from the station, windows that open and a press-button tea machine outside our door.

At rare intervals, business hotels prefer avoiding the embarrassment of foreigners, lest unruly *gaijin* antics distress others or intemperate umbrella opening splash a pristine porch. If your *hoteru* is gleaned from some chance brochure, you may need momentary adjustment to its reality on arrival. Wide angle close-ups can lend extraordinary modernist dynamism to a minor facade, or balloon your dinky double into a Ritz suite. Adequate dimensions sometimes suffer from the thoughtful addition of a couch reducing movement to sideways.

Toyohashi: The manager, taught English post-war by an Australian who stayed on, chats endlessly, marking up our local train map for gardens at Mikkabi and Inasa, bringing in his night manager to expand on the theme.

Business hotels follow a formula, but the connoisseur can come to relish their discrepancies: in a humble but ambitious *hoteru*, tiny enticements gloss their austere simplicity. Entering our room, always beside the emergency exit, we anticipate the latest minimal attempt at maximal effect. A grandiose hot water pot beside the bed (the television proudly occupying the entire dressing table) or a trouser Panapress? A heated multi-press button combination bidet/loo seat? A coffee table and armchairs? Alternatively, space for your bags. Or pick one only – liquid soap dispenser, hairdryer or welcoming cake and green tea? Ubiquitous – tooth brushes, television porn catalogue and the congenial warmth of mid-summer doonas.

Nara: A room narrower than the stairwell. Squashed above the bathroom door, 'The Beaver' air-con, too noisy for use, has a smart digital control which sets everything: clock, temperature, alarm and others – never did decipher the kanji. Only trouble, so little room that on opening the door for towelling space, a casual arm wave sets the alarm for 5.20 am . . .

The business hotel endears itself through idiosyncratic quirks amid Spartan similarity. Its practicality outweighs crawling around your luggage on a cheap *ryokan*'s tatami. Calligraphic touches of old Japan like fan and scroll lurking over the *tokonoma* television don't help to dry the washing. Fleeing ancient shoji and open-air tooth-scrub troughs, you welcome blandness, enlivened by an eighth floor close-up of nightly neon or morning exercise time in the office over the road. Although it's prosaic, tea is hotter from electric jugs than a thermos on a lacquer tray – and if you yearn for cultural difference, perhaps downstairs the foyer toilet has a paper holder that plays Piaf when pulled. *Non, je ne regrette rien.*

Kumamoto: A large rotating brush machine for shining shoes almost blocks the lobby, while excessive heating produces an early evening fire alarm. 'Kaji no!' the tremulous tourist telephoner was told. 'It happens all the time.' 'Fire' was a word luckily learnt that very day from a castle guard who'd seen Australian bushfires on television.

Most memorable are the floor mats in the Kayabacho Pearl lifts which change name with the day of the week. To assist the hung-over salaryman? There is something strangely reassuring about being greeted with 'Monday' when you step inside in the morning. Particularly if you've had an earthquake in the night.

GARDENS IN HISTORY
GLOSSARY
MAPS
BIBLIOGRAPHY
INDEX

ndividuals and institutions of power, wealth and influence created many of the gardens in this book. So intertwined are the fortunes of great families, cities, religious institutions and gardens in Japan that a correlating overview, however skimpy, seems advisable to encapsulate these historical connections. Dates of periods, a matter of some conjecture, are those adopted by the historian George Sansom and the Art Research Institute of Tokyo.

Prehistory to Nara Period: to 710 AD

History The earliest people came from mainland Asia over land bridges more than thirty thousand years ago, perhaps much earlier. They lived in scattered communities of hunter-fisher-gatherers along shorelines in pit, pole and thatch dwellings. After about 500 BC migrants from the continent introduced wet-field rice cultivation and iron and bronze technologies to western Japan. Descendants spread east, subduing occupying tribes and establishing larger settlements with more comfortable dwellings. By about 300 AD one *uji* (familial group) had achieved suzerainty over others in the Yamato plain, the region near Nara. This putative kingdom spread outwards, gradually asserting influence over Japan west of the Kanto plain and laying the foundations of the Japanese nation.

The Yamato kingdom established a colony in southern Korea in 369 AD, a connection facilitating the entry into Japan of Chinese culture and Korean immigrants, including skilled artisans such as metal workers and experts in silkworm culture.

Buddhism, formally introduced to Japan in 552 AD, won the support of the powerful Soga clan and subsequently prince Shotoku Taishi (574–622), regent to Empress Suiko (reigned 592–628). Supported by his patronage the religion spread rapidly, and with it literacy and scholarship among elites. Nakatomi no Kamatari, later to be awarded the family name of Fujiwara, ousted long-time Soga rivals in a palace coup in 645, and participated in the Taika Reform, the application of T'ang China administrative structures to Japan.

Gardens and Cultural Influences The Japanese were introduced to Chinese gardens when envoys, visiting Luoyang in 607, saw Emperor Sui Yang-ti's great Western Park under construction. China already had a long tradition of building hunting parks and pleasure gardens, such as the vast assemblage of lakes, 'mystic isles', hills and pavilions created by Emperor Han Wu-ti (reigned 140–87 BC). In 612, Empress Suiko built the first known garden in Japan, a palace garden in the Chinese style with a pond, an island and a Shumisen constructed by an immigrant Korean craftsman. Her uncle, Soga no Umako, a nobleman and patron of Buddhism, built a garden c 620 which earned him the appellation Shima no Otodo (Great Minister of the Island).

From the time of the reign of Emperor Temmu (673–686) the Grand Shrines at Ise have been built on alternate sites every twenty years (a few lapses aside). The unused site remains an open plane of gravel and is thought to be a garden archetype.

Nara Period: 710–794

History Yamato rulers chose Nara, its topography favoured by geomantic principles, as the site for the first permanent capital modelled on T'ang capital Ch'ang-an. Religion, scholarship, architecture and art, all heavily indebted to Chinese models, flourished in Japan's first great cultural flowering. The *Kojiki* (Records of Ancient Matters), completed in 712, recorded mythological origins of the nation. The *Nihon Shoki* (Chronicles of Japan) was completed in 720.

Buddhist temples, assisted by imperial land grants, eventually grew in power and influence to the point where they were seen as potential threats to imperial hegemony. A decision was taken to move the capital away from Nara.

Gardens and Cultural Influences Early gardens featured ponds, islands, rock groups, trees and flowering shrubs in the style imported from China. Later gardens, while retaining these elements, began to recall beautiful scenery encountered by nobles and priests as they travelled around the country and across the seas to China, particularly coastal scenes with pebbled shores and weathered outcrops of rocks. Until recently only poetry, as in the anthology known as *Man'yoshu* (Collection of Myriad Leaves), completed c 766, could convey the atmosphere of Nara gardens, but reconstruction work over thirty years on a site east of the old imperial palace has now brought the style vividly alive.

To-in Teien, a Nara garden.

Heian Period: 794–1185

History Emperor Kammu (reigned 781–806) founded Heiankyo (Capital of Peace and Tranquillity) on land deemed geomantically desirable and with a river link to Naniwa (near Osaka). The city (now Kyoto) was modelled on Ch'ang-an, with a street grid related to cardinal points and the palace centrally at the northern end. The Fujiwara clan manipulated the imperial family to figurehead status after the reign of Emperor Junna (reigned 823–833), acquired great wealth and political control, climaxing with the term of Michinaga (966–1027) as *kampaku* (chief advisor to the emperor).

Aristocrats embraced esoteric Buddhism, with its emphasis on the emotional appeal of colours, patterns and rituals. Fujiwara authority waned after the mid-eleventh century. Following a century of stable rule by retired ('cloistered') emperors, with puppets on the throne, the period closed in a power struggle between two great military clans, the Taira and the Minamoto.

Kajuji, founded 900.

The Taira maintained superiority for thirty years until finally defeated by Minamoto forces at Dan-no-ura in western Honshu in 1185.

Gardens and Cultural Influences The period was one of unparalleled splendour and refinement in architecture, manners, dress and arts. Aristocrats built pleasure gardens modelled on Chinese precedents, with large ponds designed for boating parties, islands, artificial hills and pavilions. The *Sakuteiki*, the first treatise on garden-making, was written by a nobleman named Tachibana no Toshitsuna in the eleventh century. With the rise in popularity of Jodo (Pure Land) Buddhism in the eleventh and twelfth centuries, gardens were built to represent Amida's Western Paradise. Basic elements were lotus ponds in front of halls housing statues of Amida.

Motsuji's paradise garden.

Kamakura Period: 1185–1392

History After the Minamoto victory, Yoritomo (1147–1199), head of the clan, moved the seat of government from Heiankyo to Kamakura, centre of the family fiefdom. He was made shogun in 1192. Following his death and some subsequent years of uncertain leadership under his heirs, the Hojo family took control and governed as regents to puppet shoguns chosen from high-ranking court families. The emperors remained powerless in Kyoto.

Mongols invaded Japan in 1274 and again in 1281, their fleets driven back each time by fortuitous storms that became known as *kamikaze*, or divine winds. Weakened by the costs of war, inadequate leadership and unrewarded, hence restive, samurai, the Kamakura government fell in 1333 to forces supporting Emperor Godaigo, and the seat of government was returned to Kyoto.

Among the emperor's supporters was a defecting Hojo vassal, Ashikaga Takauji. Emperor Godaigo proclaimed restoration of imperial rule (Kemmu Restoration), but a year later Takauji turned on him. He installed a new emperor, set up headquarters in the Muromachi district of Kyoto and, claiming descent from Minamoto Yoritomo, had himself appointed shogun. Meanwhile Godaigo withdrew to set up court in the Yoshino district south of Kyoto and near Nara, where he died in 1339.

Rivalry between the southern and northern courts ended in 1392 when the southern emperor returned to Kyoto, relinquishing imperial claims. Takauji's grandson Yoshimitsu was shogun at the time, and a new cultural flowering was under way.

Tokoji

Tenryuji

Saihoji

Gardens and Cultural Influences **Zen Buddhism** was brought to Japan from China during the Kamakura period, initially by the priest Eisai (1141–1215), who also introduced tea for cultivation, and other priests. Their Zen was a hybrid form combined with esoteric practices; pure Sung-style Zen was introduced by the Chinese priest Rankei Doryu (1213–1278) who arrived in Japan in 1246. With the assistance of fifth regent, Hojo Tokiyori (1226–1263), Rankei founded Kenchoji in 1253. From this time, aided by the arrival of Chinese priests fleeing Mongol invasions, Japanese priests visiting China and the enthusiastic support of the warrior class, Zen flourished, spread and permeated other cultural activities, particularly garden-making.

Zen gardens were designed in the 'contemplation' style, to be viewed from inside a building during meditation: a period example can be seen at Tokoji, the temple Rankei converted during a period of exile from Kamakura. They also featured Chinese themes, such as the *ryumonbaku* seen at Tenryuji.

The most famous priest connected with gardens was Muso Soseki (1275–1351), also known as Muso Kokushi (National Teacher), the 'rock-placing priest' of whom it was said 'gardens are his habit'. He is considered to have designed modifications to the Tenryuji and Saihoji gardens, but was probably too busy as a teacher to have personally designed the other fifty-odd gardens attributed to him.

Muromachi Period: 1392–1568

Kinkakuji, built 1394.

History Ashikaga dominance continued for two strife-ridden centuries. A shogunate succession dispute conducted by two hereditary vassal families, the Hosokawa and the Yamana, led to the Onin War (1467–1477), during which time Kyoto was reduced to ashes. Aristocrats fled to safer places such as Yamaguchi and Sakai (south of Osaka). Fighting broke out all over the country while the imperial line remained in Kyoto, enfeebled and impoverished. The time between 1467 and 1573 is known as Sengoku (Country at War).

Ginkakuji

Ryoanji

Joeiji

The first westerners known to enter Japan were Portuguese whose vessel was driven ashore at Tanegashima in 1542. From this flowed the introduction of firearms and the arrival of Christian missionaries, notably the Jesuit Francis Xavier who landed at Kagoshima in 1549.

Warlord Oda Nobunaga (1534–1582), who had exploited the use of firearms and subdued a region around Owari province (in present-day Aichi prefecture), marched on Kyoto in 1568. Five years later the last Ashikaga shogun fled the capital.

Gardens and Cultural Influences The Muromachi period was one of extraordinary cultural development despite political tensions, wars and famines. Art works from the Sung and Yuan dynasties entered Japan. Zen Buddhism continued to thrive. These influences joined a fusion of courtly culture and warrior vigour to inspire gardens of exceptional beauty and artistry.

Early aristocrats' gardens looked back to the golden age of the Heian Period, as at Kinkakuji. *Karesansui* gardens made their appearance at Zen temples.

Two important artists are connected with gardens during this period. Sesshu Toyo (1420–1506) is regarded as the greatest master of Japanese ink landscape painting. He travelled and studied in China between 1467 and 1469. On his return, he built Kyu Kameishi-bo and Joeiji in western Japan, and Sesshuji in Kyoto. Soami (died 1525) mastered the Southern Sung style of painting. He painted door panels at Daisen-in, so is thought to have influenced its garden. Ryoanji and Ginkakuji are also sometimes attributed to him.

Momoyama Period: 1568–1615

History Oda Nobunaga ruthlessly unified central Japan. He built Japan's first great feudal castle, Azuchi-jo by Lake Biwa, but took his own life in 1582 after being ambushed by a trusted lieutenant while in Honnoji in Kyoto. Toyotomi Hideyoshi (1536–1598), Nobunaga's top lieutenant in the field, returned from campaigning to Kyoto, defeated Nobunaga's attackers, and took command. Hideyoshi was appointed *kampaku* by the emperor in 1585 and continued the process of national unification from the luxurious Fushimi-jo he built in the Momoyama district south of Kyoto. In 1592 he launched an attack on China through Korea; the campaign was abandoned after his death.

Senshukaku Teien – a lord's garden of the Momoyama period.

Hideyoshi died of natural causes in 1598, entrusting his only surviving son, five-year-old Hideyori, to a council of five elders. Rivalries among these daimyo guardians was resolved in the Battle of Sekigahara in 1600, when Tokugawa Ieyasu (1546–1616), whose domain included the entire Kanto plain, was victorious. Ieyasu was made shogun in 1603, then abdicated in favour of his son Hidetada two years later without relinquishing his authority. In 1615 Ieyasu laid siege to Osaka-jo, the castle where Hideyori and his mother had been permitted to reside, forcing their suicides.

Zen restraint at Koto-in.

Gardens and Cultural Influences Gardens of the period are characterised by opposing styles, the vigorous and opulent creations of feudal lords on one hand, and the delicately understated tea ceremony gardens and Zen temple gardens influenced by tea on the other.

The most famous period figure connected with the tea ceremony is Sen no Rikyu (1522–1591), who studied at Juko-in at Daitokuji. He became the greatest of all tea masters, influencing the design of tea houses and gardens. He established principles of ritual and deportment known as Sado (the Way of Tea), and was tea master to Nobunaga and Hideyoshi. His life ended when Hideyoshi forced him to commit suicide over a perceived insult.

Edo Period: 1615–1867

History The Tokugawa shogunate, based in Edo, set in place measures designed to emasculate potential opposition and ensure stability. Tokugawa domains covered about a fourth of Japan, while the rest of the country was supervised by two hundred and fifty-odd daimyo. Daimyo were required to set up house in Edo and spend half their time there, leaving their wives and heirs behind as virtual hostages when they returned to their domains.

Society was peaceful, prosperous, warrior-dominated, hierarchical (descending in status from samurai, through farmer and artisan to merchant) and regulated in almost all aspects of daily life.

Suspicious of Christian missionaries' intent, and fearful that foreign traders would empower opponents, the rulers banned Christianity and closed the country's doors to foreigners with one exception – Dutch and Chinese traders were permitted to operate out of Nagasaki harbour.

Social and economic conditions could not be eternally frozen. Various factors, such as an emerging capitalist class, rural disquiet, education, questioning of the shogunate's suzerainty regarding imperial primacy, vulnerability to external threats and, ultimately, the arrival of American Commodore Perry's ships in 1853, followed by the friendship treaty of 1854 and the opening of treaty ports, undermined the shogunate to the point of collapse. This occurred when a coalition of western feudatories united under the chrysanthemum flag of the imperial house and, after several months of unrest, the last Tokugawa shogun surrendered his powers to the youthful Emperor Meiji in November 1867.

Enshu's Konchi-in.

Chishaku-in

Gardens and Cultural Influences At Katsura villa between 1615–1645, Prince Toshihito and his son created the first great stroll garden. Retired Emperor Gomizuno-o followed with Sento Gosho and Shugakuin.

In the design of Sento Gosho, Gomizuno-o was assisted by Kobori Enshu (1579–1647), regarded as Japan's finest landscape architect. Also a tea master, he designed or influenced many of the period's finest gardens including Konchi-in and Koho-an. So pervasive was his influence that many gardens not directly connected to him are said to be in 'Enshu style'. He is also credited with the bold *o-karikomi* style of garden seen at Raikyuji and Daichiji.

Daimyo families built stroll gardens in Edo and in their home fiefs, sometimes over several generations and vast when resources allowed.

The Tokugawa regime assisted the reconstruction of some temples destroyed in earlier wars, resulting in some of the period's more important gardens (the Nanzenji complex and Chishaku-in). Many temple gardens were constructed in this long stable period, but with a tendency to stereotyping as it progressed. Some scholars found ways to demonstrate their intellectual independence from Tokugawa conformism through building gardens in the so-called 'literary man's style', actually an absence of recognised style. Shisendo is the prime example.

Edo period stroll gardens

Shugakuin Imperial Villa

Sento Gosho

Katsura Imperial Villa

Rikugien

Ritsurin Park

Suizenji Park

Meiji Period: 1868–1912

History Emperor Meiji re-established imperial rule in 1868. In 1869 he moved the court to Tokyo (Eastern Capital), as the former Edo would be henceforth known, and converted the Tokugawa shogun's castle into the palace. An oligarchy of men from western clans formed the new government, which embarked upon a program of modernisation in a drive to establish equality with western powers.

Feudalism was abolished, lords surrendered their fiefs, the country was divided into prefectures administered by governors appointed in Tokyo, samurai took off their swords and found employment in bureaucracies or survived on small pensions. Harbours, railroads, banks, post offices, telegraph offices and printing presses reflected the infrastructures and edifices of western material culture.

On 11 February 1889 the emperor handed over the first written Constitution of Japan to the prime minister, and an elected assembly, albeit limited to voters representing about one per cent of the population, was established within a bicameral Diet. The industrial revolution set in during the last decade of the nineteenth century, and the period closed with the country engaging in profitable military and navy sorties against China and Russia on the continent and renewed confidence at home.

Kiyosumi Garden

Murin-an

Heian Shrine

Gardens and Cultural Influences With the abandonment of feudal administration, many great daimyo gardens were turned into public parks, for example Kenrokuen (Kanazawa) – 1871, Suizenji Park (Kumamoto) – 1879, and Korakuen (Okayama) – 1884.

Economic liberalisation allowed men in commerce to amass great fortunes and spend them in ways not allowed their low-status predecessors in the Edo period, but the gardens they made merely echoed feudal prototypes. Many gardens showed a tendency towards naturalism on one hand or formalism on the other, with a new emphasis on plants. Some gardens juxtaposed traditionally styled gardens with formal European gardens, while some, notably those connected to the professional landscape gardener Ogawa Jihei, creatively fused the two traditions.

Americans and Europeans introduced Japanese gardens to the west through writings, notably Edward S. Morse's *Japanese Homes and Their Surroundings* published in 1886, Josiah Conder's *Landscape Gardening in Japan*, published in 1893, and the writings of Lafcadio Hearn.

Taisho Period: 1912–1926, Showa Period: 1926–1989, Heisei Period: 1989–

History The first half of the twentieth century in Japan began with the 'golden' glow of the late Meiji period, and ended in domestic devastation brought about by expansionist policies pursued by militarist powers. This complicated time is described succinctly in Richard Storry's *A History of Modern Japan*.

Along the way the country profited from a war boom (1914–1918) and endured the subsequent collapse, saw its most populous city destroyed in the Great Kanto Earthquake of 1923, joined the rest of the world in the Great Depression beginning in 1930, and nurtured a rising tide of nationalism. The Japanese army overran Manchuria in 1931–32 and installed a puppet emperor, naming the new state Manchukuo.

Japan entered into hostilities with China in 1937 and into the Pacific War with the attack on Pearl Harbour on 7 December 1941. The war ended after the USA dropped atomic bombs on Hiroshima and Nagasaki. American occupation followed, a new constitution was prepared, and the emperor renounced imperial claims to divinity. The

Domon Ken Kinenkan

Adachi Museum

Tofukuji Hojo

country showed extraordinary resilience in its recovery from this period of destruction and humiliation to become an economic super-power in the latter half of the twentieth century.

Gardens and Cultural Influences Knowledge of Japanese art, architecture and gardens became widely disseminated throughout the western world, to the point that the 'Japanese' garden became a generic type built anywhere. Conversely, the aesthetics of western modernism infiltrated Japan, beginning with the arts and extending to architecture and landscape design, particularly after the second world war. Its pre-war influence can be seen in gardens Shigemori Mirei designed for the Tofukuji Hojo in 1938. One of the period's outstanding figures, a scholar, researcher and writer as well as an active designer, Shigemori in 1939 published twenty-six volumes of research material including measured drawings of existing gardens, and has been the major influence on modern analytical thought. Meanwhile, Nakane Kinsaku continued the traditional mode in fine gardens, as at the Jonangu Shrine and the Adachi Museum.

Excellent modern gardens can be found all over the country in commercial premises and museums, such as the Domon Ken Kinenkan. New levels of minimalism and abstraction can be seen in some recent 'gardens' using neither plant life nor natural materials other than water, as at the Shonandai Cultural Centre.

Amida	Compassionate Amida Buddha of Jodo, the Pure Land in the West where followers believed they would be transported for an after-life of everlasting bliss through repetition of a simple prayer of homage. Represented in statues in Amida halls overlooking 'paradise gardens'.
bijutsukan	Art museum
bodhisattva	A Buddhist saint who has postponed his own Nirvana in order to save all sentient beings.
cha-no-yu	Tea ceremony
chozubachi	Handwashing basin, usually stone. Originally used in temples and shrines for ritual purification, later introduced into tea gardens with a ladle for rinsing mouths and often set low so that users must stoop. Taller variations followed, with a more general application in traditional gardens.
cryptomeria	*Cryptomeria japonica*, or Japanese cedar (a tall growing conifer).
daimyo	Feudal lord
engawa	Verandah-like timber-boarded floor structure between rooms and garden. A transition between 'inner' and 'outer'.
feng-shui	Ancient Chinese ordinances governing the siting and design of dwellings, settlements etc to accord propitiously with forces held to be present in nature.
geomancy	Western term for *feng-shui*.
gozan	'Five mountains'. Ranking system applied to Zen temples in Kamakura period, originally five in Kamakura and five in Kyoto. Present-day *gozan* temples in Kyoto are Nanzenji, Tofukuji, Kenninji, Shokokuji and Tenryuji.
hako-zukuri	Topiary in box shapes.
hojo	Chief priest's (or abbot's) quarters in a Buddhist temple.
hondo	Main hall in a Buddhist temple.
Horai (Mt)	Mountain dwelling of the immortals. Often represented in gardens by rock formations. Also known as *horai* rock, *horai* mountain, *horaisan*.
ike, o-ike	Pond
-in	Sub-temple in a Buddhist temple precinct, e.g. Daisen-in.
iwakura	'Rock seat', a rock worshipped for the presence of a deity.
-ji, tera, dera	Buddhist temple, e.g. Daitokuji, Miidera.
jinja, jingu, -gu	Shinto shrine
Jizo	Saviour deity, especially for children. Also travellers' guardian.
-jo	Castle
kaisando	Founder's hall in a temple, enshrining the founder's ashes.
kamejima	Turtle island
kamedejima	Turtle peninsula
kami	At the heart of Shinto (Way of the Gods). *Kami* are sacred spirits invested in ancestors, exceptional living beings and awe-inspiring natural phenomena (such as growth, fertility and production, wind and thunder, sun, mountains, rivers, trees and rocks), thus rendering them subjects of adoration and worship.
kampaku	Chief adviser to the emperor, highest court position below emperor from 882 to 1868. At times the *kampaku* effectively ruled in the emperor's name, as with heads of the Fujiwara family in the middle Heian period. Toyotomi Hideyoshi, unable to claim the correct lineage to be shogun, was appointed *kampaku*.

Kano school	Family-based school of painters founded by Kano Masanobu (1434–1530) mingling Chinese and *yamato-e* styles; expanded into a powerful, prosperous painting atelier by his son Motonobu (1476–1559), with a distinctive style of carefully categorised brushwork for unifying assistants' work. Major force in Momoyama art. Apogee reached with Eitoku (1543–1590).
karedaki, karetaki	Dry waterfall, constructed as such. Common feature in Zen gardens including pond gardens, where they are often made with rocks massed on rising land above a pond.
karesansui	'Withered mountain water'. Waterless garden. Sand, gravel or small pebbles are often used to imply a pond or a stream.
karikomi, o-karikomi	Topiary applied to hedges.
kawaramono	River-dwelling labourers who worked on gardens, and from whose ranks the first professional gardeners came.
koan	A riddle, with no rational solution, put by a Zen master to his students in their search for enlightenment.
koen	Park, public garden
koto	Stringed musical instrument.
-maru	Fortress, enclosure
mikiri	Trimming
mon	Gate
nakajima	Central island in a pond.
night mooring stones	Row of stones across a pond, said to resemble a line of moored junks in a safe harbour.
nijiriguchi	Tiny 'wriggling-in' entrance to a tea house, designed to impose a mood of humility and receptiveness among tea ceremony participants.
o-	An honorific prefix, eg *o-karikomi*, to show respect.
rigyoseki	Rock representing a carp attempting to ascend a waterfall.
rikushu-no-matsu	'Boat pine', a pine tree trained to resemble the hull and sail of a junk. There is a fine example at Kinkakuji.
roji	'Dewy path'. The garden leading to a tea house.
ryumonbaku	Garden waterfall representing Ryumon (Dragon Gate) Falls in China, grouped with a *rigyoseki* (see above).
sabi	Patina. Implies essential elegance with overtones only age can produce. Associated with *wabi*.
san, zan	Mountain
sansui	Mountain and water
sanzon	Sacred triad, referring in rock groups to a composition with a larger central rock flanked by two smaller ones, symbolising a Buddha between two *bodhisattvas*. Often seen in the compounds *sanzon-ishigumi* and *sanzon-iwagumi* (Deity triad rock group).
shakkei	Borrowed scenery
shimenawa	Straw ropes around sacred area.
shinden	'Hall for sleeping'. The main hall at the centre of a Heian period mansion.
shinden style	Typical mansion and garden architecture of the Heian period. Central hall with corridors extending both sides past a gravel area into a southern pond garden.

shogun	Common abbreviation of *seiitaishogun* 'barbarian-subduing great general', the title originally bestowed by the emperor upon generals who led expeditions into northern Japan c 800; later on leaders of the Minamoto, Ashikaga and Tokugawa families who governed Japan in the emperor's name. In acquiring the title, founders of both latter regimes claimed Minamoto descendence.
shoin	'Writing hall'. The name of a corner room in an abbot's quarters used for study or conversation. Later also a room or building for special guests.
shoin style	Structures developed during the Muromachi period, typically having a room with all or some of the following features: *tokonoma* (decorative alcove), staggered shelves, built-in desk, decorative doors. Also with *tatami* covered floors, *fusuma* (painted or unpainted sliding screens between rooms) and shoji (see below) protected by sliding panels. The style adopted by the samurai class.
shoji	Translucent sliding external screen made with paper fixed to timber lattice.
Shumisen	Mountain at the centre of the universe, derived from Hindu cosmology – also known as Mt Meru.
sukiya style	A development of *shoin* style under the influence of tea house architecture in the Momoyama period. The genre of rural architecture transformed into high style, characterised by elegant and refined simplicity, exemplified at Katsura.
teien	Garden (also *niwa*)
tobi-ishi	Stepping stones
torii	Entrance gate to a Shinto shrine precinct, traditionally made in wood or stone with characteristic double beams.
tsubo-niwa	Small courtyard garden
tsukiyama	Artificial mountain, commonly made with soil excavated during pond construction.
tsurudejima	Crane peninsula
tsurujima	Crane island
uji	Aristocratic familial group (clan).
wabi	Subdued taste. Implies the unity of elegance and casualness, the sumptuous within the simple. Associated with *sabi*.
yama, san, zan	Mountain
yamato-e	Distinctive Japanese painting style that evolved during the late Heian period, a time when Japan was relatively isolated from China. Characterised by references to themes in Japanese poetry and literature, colour, expressions of the intimate and lush nature of Japanese landscape, the four seasons and a sense of *mono-no-aware* (pathos, the tears underlying life: the 'ah-ness' of things).
yamabuki	*Kerria japonica*, a plant especially suited to marsh-pond landscapes.
yatsuhashi	Zig-zag bridge, commonly across iris beds.
yin/yang	Symbiotic opposites at the heart of ancient Chinese cosmology. Yin: female, dark, passive etc. Yang: male, bright, active etc.
zazenseki	Zen meditation or prayer stone.

GARDENS EAST AND NORTH OF KYOTO

E1 Motsuji
E2 Domon Ken Kinenkan
E3 Homma Bijutsukan
E4 Gyokusenji
E5 Shimizuen
E6 Ganjoji
E7 Kairakuen
E8 Noninji
E9 Rikugien
E10 Korakuen
E11 Hama Rikyu Garden
E12 Kiyosumi Garden
E13 Nezu Institute of Fine Arts
E14 Meiji Shrine Iris Garden
E15 Imperial Palace East Garden
E16 Horikiri Shobuen
E17 Kenchoji
E18 Shonandai Cultural Centre
E19 Tokoji
E20 Erinji
E21 Ryutanji
E22 Makayaji
E23 Eihoji
E24 Urakuen
E25 Kenrokuen
E26 Gyokusenen
E27 Nomura Residence Garden

E28 Heisenji
E29 Asakura Family
     Residential Ruins
E30 Shibata Residence Garden
E31 Saifukuji
E32 Daitsuji
E33 Genkyuen
E34 Ryotanji
E35 Daichiji
E36 Enman-in
E37 Koshoji
E38 Jizo-in
E39 Isuien
E40 To-in Teien
     (East Palace Garden)
E41 Jiko-in
E42 Joruriji

Hiraizumi E1
Sakata E2, E3
Haguro E4
Shibata E5
Niigata
Iwaki E6
Kanazawa E25–E27
Mito E7
Fukui
Katsuyama E28
Ichijodani E29
Hanno E8
Tokyo E9–E16
Kofu E19
Enzan E20
Tsuruga E30, E31
Nagahama E32
Inuyama E24
Shonandai E18
Kutsuki E37
Tajimi E23
Hikone E33, E34
Nagoya
Kamakura E17
Kyoto
Minakuchi
Mikkabi E22
Kiga E21
Otsu E36
Daichiji E35
Nara E39–E42
Seki E38
Ise

N

INDIVIDUAL MAPS – GARDENS EAST AND NORTH OF KYOTO

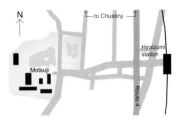

E1 Hiraizumi

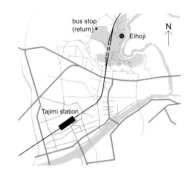

E23 Tajimi

E35 Minakuchi

E5 Shibata

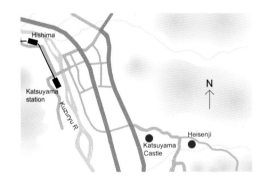

E28 Katsuyama

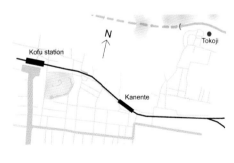

E19 Kofu

E30 Tsuruga

TOKYO

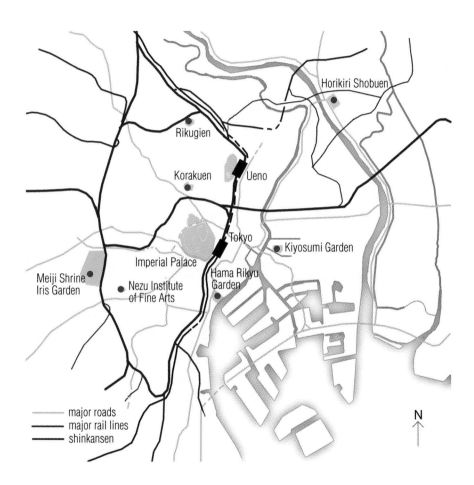

Horikiri Shobuen

Rikugien

Korakuen   Ueno

Tokyo

Kiyosumi Garden

Imperial Palace

Meiji Shrine
Iris Garden   Nezu Institute   Hama Rikyu
of Fine Arts   Garden

—— major roads
—— major rail lines
—— shinkansen

N

KYOTO GARDENS

1	Sanzen-in	14	Murin-an	27	Koho-an	40	Koetsuji
2	Jakko-in	15	Kodaiji	28	Daisen-in	41	Kinkakuji
3	Rengeji	16	Chishaku-in	29	Zuiho-in	42	Ryoanji
4	Shugakuin Imperial Villa	17	Fumon-in	30	Ryogen-in	43	Ninnaji
5	Manshu-in	18	Tofukuji Hojo	31	Koto-in	44	Toji-in
6	Shisendo	19	Sesshuji	32	Honpoji	45	Taizo-in
7	Ginkakuji	20	Kajuji	33	Sento Gosho	46	Keishun-in
8	Hakusasonso	21	Sambo-in	34	Nijo Castle	47	Osawa Pond
9	Heian Shrine	22	Jonangu Shrine	35	Shinsenen	48	Tenryuji
10	Nanzenji Hojo	23	Byodo-in	36	Nishi Honganji	49	Saihoji
11	Nanzen-in	24	Shuon-an	37	Shoseien	50	Katsura Imperial Villa
12	Tenju-an	25	Garden of Fine Art	38	Entsuji		
13	Konchi-in	26	Juko-in	39	Shodenji		

Kinkakuji

KYOTO GARDENS

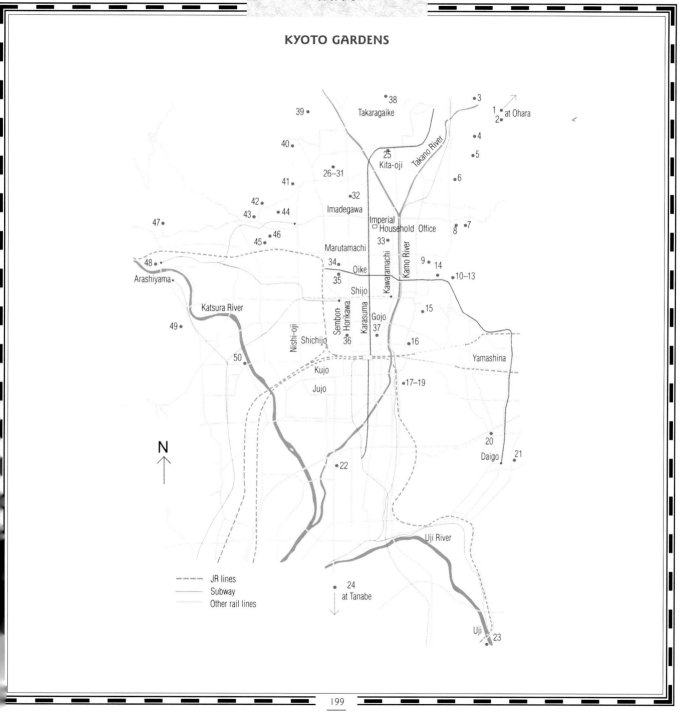

GARDENS WEST AND SOUTH OF KYOTO

W1   Fumon-in
W2   Kongobuji
W3   Momijidani Garden
W4   Kishiwada Castle Garden
W5   Honpukuji (Mizumi-do)
W6   Kozenji
W7   Korakuen
W8   Tokoen
W9   Achi Shrine
W10   Raikyuji
W11   Ritsurin Park
W12   Chikurin-in
W13   Senshukaku Teien
W14   Hokokuji

W15   Fukada Residence
W16   Adachi Museum Gardens
W17   Kokokuji
W18   Shukkeien
W19   Tsuki no Katsura Garden
W20   Mori Residence
W21   Joeiji
W22   Ikoji
W23   Mampukuji
W24   Kyu Kameishi-bo

W25   Komyoji
W26   Suizenji Park (Jojuen)
W27   Chiran Samurai Residences
W28   Iso Teien

INDIVIDUAL MAPS – GARDENS WEST AND SOUTH OF KYOTO

W1 Koyasan

W12 Tokushima

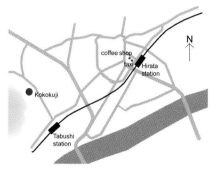

W17 Hirata

W19 Hofu

W15 Yonago

W22 Masuda

As well as pamphlets and brochures from temples and other gardens we have visited, we have obtained information and clarification from the following publications, particularly the works of Professor Günter Nitschke, Loraine Kuck, Yoshikawa Isao, and Marc Tribe and Ron Herman, all of which have urged us into further discoveries.

BOOKS ON GARDENS

Bring, Mitchell and Wayemburgh, Josse. *Japanese Gardens: Design and Meaning*. New York: McGraw-Hill Book Company, 1981. (McGraw-Hill Series in Landscape and Landscape Architecture, Albert Fein Consulting ed.)

Conder, Josiah. *Landscape Gardening in Japan*. New York: Dover Publications, 1964. 1893 text re-published.

Hibi, Sadao, with introduction by Yoshikawa Isao. *A Celebration of Japanese Gardens*. Tokyo: Graphic-sha, 1994.

Harada, Jiro, ed. by Holme, Geoffrey. *The Gardens of Japan*. London: The Studio Ltd, 1928.

Itoh, Teiji. *The Gardens of Japan*. Tokyo and New York: Kodansha International, 1984.

Itoh, Teiji. *Space and Illusion in the Japanese Garden*, New York, Tokyo, Kyoto: Weatherhill/Tankosha, 1988 ed.

Keswick, Maggie. *The Chinese Garden*. London: Academy Editions 1978. New York: St Martin's Press, 1986.

Keane, Marc P. *Japanese Garden Design*: Rutland, Vermont and Tokyo: Charles E. Tuttle Co, 1996.

Kuck, Loraine. *The World of the Japanese Garden: From Chinese Origins to Modern Landscape Art*. New York and Tokyo: Weatherhill, 1984.

Mizuno, Katsuhiko. *The Gardens of Kyoto - 1. The Celebrated Gardens of the Western, Northern and Southern Areas. And 2. The Celebrated Gardens of the Central and Eastern Areas*. Kyoto: Kyoto Shoin Co Ltd, 1987.

Nakane, Kinsaku, trans. Hickman, Money L. and Minobe, Kaichi. *Kyoto Gardens*. Osaka: Hoikusha, 22nd edition 1992.

Nitschke, Günter. *Japanese Gardens (The Architecture of the Japanese Garden: Right Angle and Natural Form)*. Köln: Benedikt Taschen, 1991.

Nitschke, Günter. *From Shinto to Ando*. London and Berlin: Academy Editions/Ernst and Sohn, 1993.

Rimer, T. et al. *Shisendo – Hall of the Poetry Immortals*. New York: Weatherhill, and Tokyo: Tanko-Weatherhill, 1991.

Slawson, David. *A Secret Teachings in the Art of Japanese Gardens*. Tokyo, New York: Kodansha International, 1987.

Takakuwa, Gisei (commentary) and Asano, Kiichi (photographs). *Japanese Gardens Revisited*. Rutland Vermont and Tokyo: Charles E. Tuttle Co, 1973.

Treib, Mark and Herman, Ron. *A Guide to the Gardens of Kyoto*. Tokyo: Shufunotomo Company, Ltd, 1980.

Wright, Tom and Mizuno, Katsuhiko, photographs. *Zen Gardens, Kyoto's Nature Enclosed*. Kyoto: Suiko Books,1994.

Yoshikawa, Isao. *Stone Basins: the Accents of Japanese Gardens*. Tokyo: Graphic-sha, 1989.

Yoshikawa, Isao. *The World of Zen Gardens*. Tokyo: Graphic-sha, 1991.

GUIDE BOOKS

Cooper M. *Exploring Kamakura*. New York, Tokyo: Weatherhill, 1983.

Iris Co Ltd production. *Japan: a Bilingual Atlas*. Tokyo, New York, London: Kodansha International, 1991.

Kinoshita, June and Palevsky, Nicholas. *Gateway to Japan*. Tokyo and New York: Kodansha International, 1990.

Mosher, Gouverneur. *Kyoto, A Contemplative Guide*. Rutland, Vermont and Tokyo: Charles E. Tuttle Co, 1964.

Taylor C., Strauss R. and Wheeler T. *Japan, a Lonely Planet Travel Survival Kit*. Melbourne: Lonely Planet Publications, 5th Ed. 1994.

Ward, Phillip. *Cultural, Historical, and Artistic Guide to Nara, Kyoto, and Tokyo*. England, Cambridge: The Oleander Press, 1985.

OTHER READING

Ashihara, Yoshinobu. *The Aesthetic Townscape*. London, and Cambridge, Mass: MIT Press, 1983.

Bognar, Botond. *The New Japanese Architecture*. New York: Rizzoli Publications, 1990.

Bognar, Botond. *The Japan Guide*. New York: Princeton Architectural Press, 1995.

Coaldrake, William. *Architecture and Authority in Japan*: London: Routledge, 1996.

Cranston, Edwin A., trans. *A Waka Anthology, Volume One: The Gem-Glistening Cup*, Stanford: Stanford University Press, 1993.

Dal Co, Francesco. *Tadao Ando* London: Phaidon Press Ltd, 1995.

Davids, Kenneth. *The Coffee Book* The Oil Mills, Weybridge, Surrey: Whittet Books Ltd, 1980.

Fairbank, John King. *China a New History*: Cambridge, Mass. and London: Belknap Press of Harvard University Press, 1994.

Goodrich, L Carrington. *A Short History of the Chinese People*: London: George Allen and Unwin Ltd, 1957, 1969.

Henshall, K.G. *A Guide to Remembering Japanese Characters*. Rutland, Vermont and Tokyo: Charles E. Tuttle Co, 1988.

Kojima, Takashi. *Written on Water: Five Hundred Poems from the Man'yoshu*: Rutland, Vermont and Tokyo: Charles E. Tuttle Co, 1995.

Kolpas, N. *Coffee*. Twickenham, England: Felix Gluck Press, 1977.

Leggett, Trevor compiled and trans. *A First Zen Reader*: Rutland, Vermont and Tokyo: Charles E. Tuttle Co, 1960.

Mason, R.H.P, and Caiger, J.G. *A History of Japan*: North Melbourne: Charles E. Tuttle Co, as imprint of Periplus Editions (HK) by arrangement with Cassell Australia, Ltd, 1997; first published Tuttle, 1973.

Morse, Edward S. *Japanese Homes and Their Surroundings*: Rutland, Vermont and Tokyo: Charles E Tuttle Co, 1973.

Murasaki, Shikibu trans. Seidensticker Edward G. *The Tale of Genji*. London: Penguin Books, 1981.

Nelson, Andrew N. *The Original Modern Reader's Japan-English Character Dictionary*. Rutland Vermont and Tokyo: Charles E Tuttle Co, Classic Edition, 1995.

Nishi, Kazuo and Hozumi, Kazuo, trans. Horton, H Mack. *What is Japanese Architecture?* Tokyo and New York: Kodansha International Ltd, first English ed.1985.

Ono, Sokyo, in collab. with Woodward, William P. *Shinto, the Kami Way*. Rutland, Vermont and Tokyo: Charles E. Tuttle Co, 1962.

Sansom, George. *A History of Japan.1334-1615*. Stanford: Stanford University Press, 1961.

Stanley-Baker, Joan. *Japanese Art*. London: Thames and Hudson Ltd, 1984.

Smith, Henry D. the 2nd, and Poster, Amy G. *Hiroshige. One Hundred Famous Views of Edo*. London: Thames and Hudson, 1986.

Storry, Richard. *A History of Modern Japan*. London: Penguin 1960.

Takeda, Tsuneo. *Kano Eitoku*. Tokyo, New York and San Francisco: Kodansha International Ltd, 1977. (First published: vol 94 of series *Nihon no bijutsu* Tokyo; Shibundo, 1974.)

Takahashi, Yasuo. *The Electric Geisha*. Tokyo and New York: Kodansha International and Kodansha America, 1994.

Totman, Conrad. *Japan before Perry*. Berkeley, Los Angeles and London: University of California Press, 1981.

Waley, Arthur. *Chinese Poems*, Dover Publications. First published London: George Allen and Unwin, 1948.

Waley, Paul. *Tokyo Now and Then, An Explorer's Guide*. New York, Tokyo: Weatherhill, 1984.

Numbers in bold indicate page numbers for main garden descriptions. Numbers in italics indicate page numbers for garden illustrations other than those associated with main garden descriptions. Garden elements that occur frequently in main garden descriptions, such as *horai* rock, *horai* island etc, are indexed only when depicted in accompanying illustrations.